Joyful Pages
Adventures in Art Journaling

Judith Cassel-Mamet

Adventure Journal Press
Denver, Colorado

ISBN: 978-0-9983141-3-6

Adventure Journal Press
PO Box 460684
Denver, CO 80246

Developmental Editor: Janice Brewster, www.creativegirlfriendspress.com
Cover and Book Designer: Karen Sulmonetti, www.sulmonettidesign.com

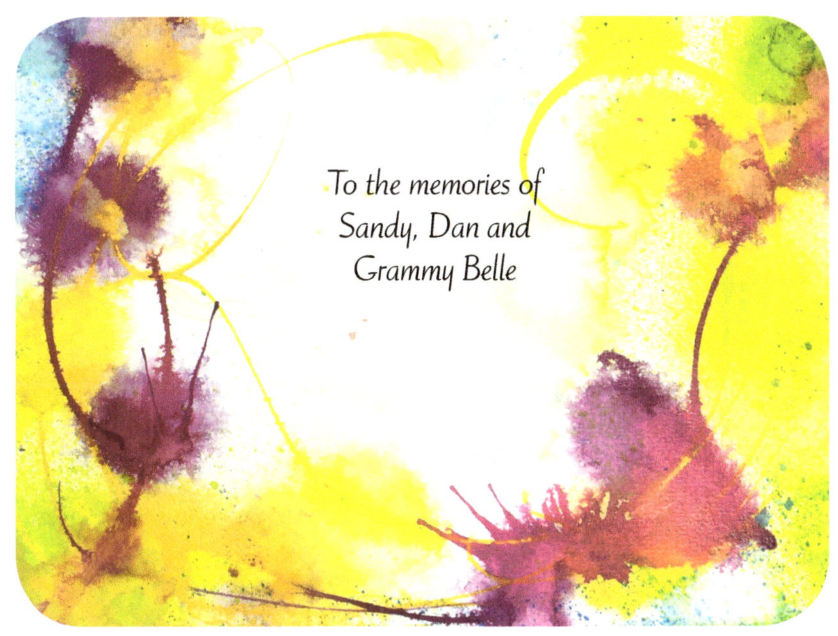

To the memories of
Sandy, Dan and
Grammy Belle

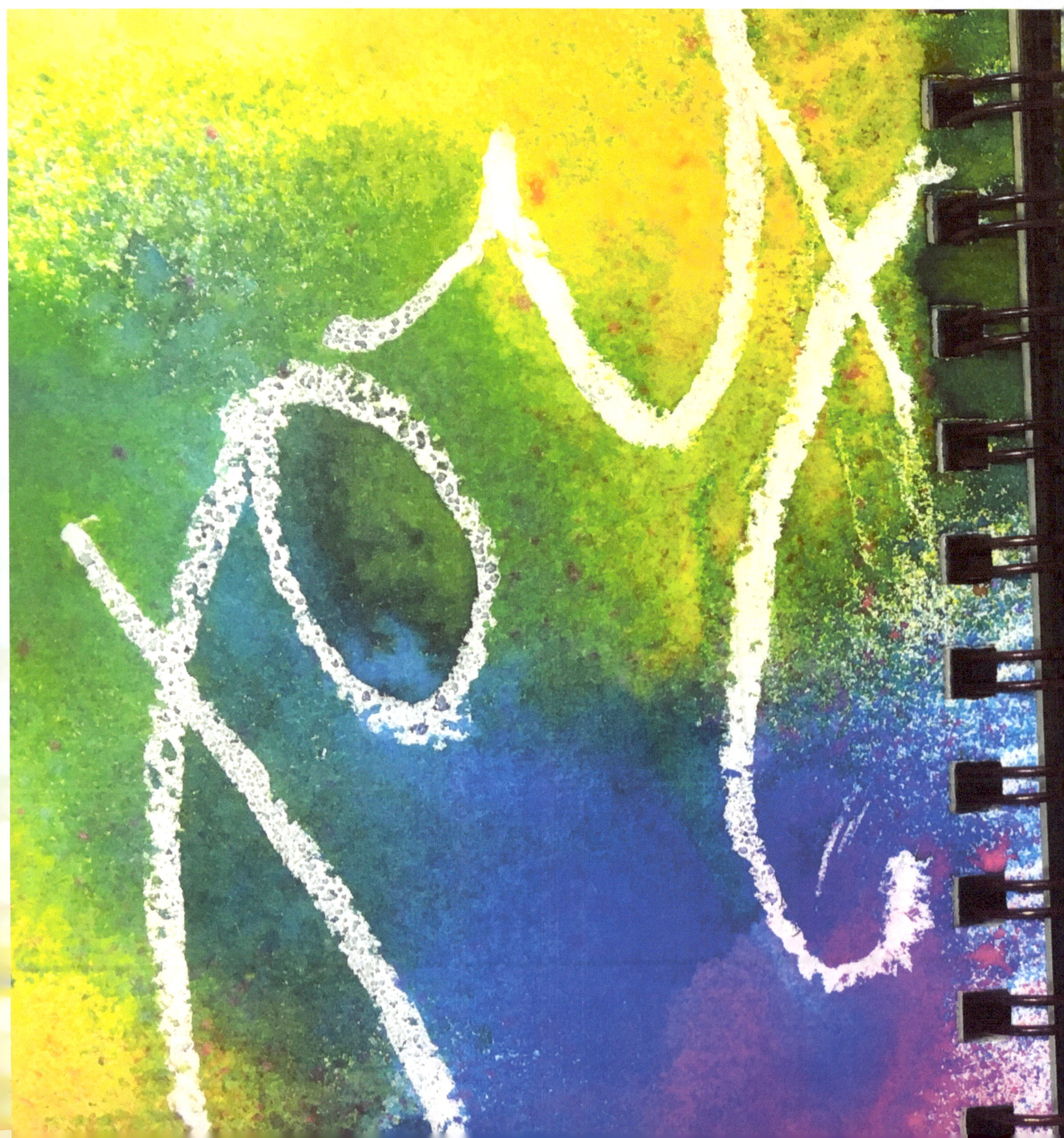

contents

1. Discover Art Journaling 6

Finding the Joy
2. Journaling in the Creative Zone 12
3. Supplies for the Journey 20

Basic Techniques and First Layers
4. Bloom and Spritz with India Inks 38
5. Spray and Splash with Dye Inks 50
6. Chalk Surprises 60

Second Layers and Beyond
7. Collaborations: Chalk + Ink + Stamps 70
8. Text as a Layer 92

Preparation Pays Off
9. Capturing Moments with Prepared Pages 104
10. Adventures in Art Journaling 114

Resources 122
   Supplies
   Sources
   Helpful Tutorials
   Further Reading
   Acknowledgments
   About the Author

1

Discover Art Journaling

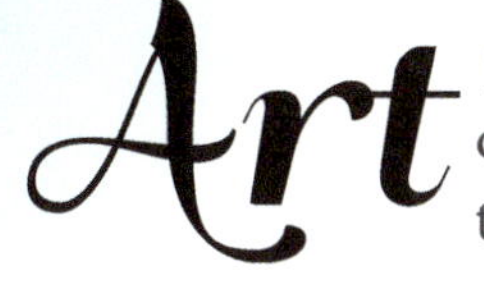

Art journaling is a form of creative expression that allows you to break every rule and be free of any pressure to produce something "beautiful." It incorporates a mixed media approach, which means you can use lots of different materials to make a page satisfying, or you can stick to just a few favorite pens. Anything goes! It is a practice that appeals to beginners and experienced artists alike, as well as folks who have never considered themselves anywhere on the artistic spectrum. Art journaling often combines visual aspects (color, texture, shapes, lines, etc.) with some text (legible or not) and usually incorporates rich, luscious layers on some pages, but the most important aspect of this work is that it reflects you and where you are in an authentic way.

Art journaling has very few rules, maybe even none. Whatever rules are presented should be considered only tools. When I teach art journaling I intentionally use the terms "suggestions or invitations" when demonstrating a technique so students don't even hear the term "rules." Some techniques you may wish to embrace; some you may not want to pick up at all. The main goal is to put something down on a page in your journal then turn that page... and to not get caught up in aiming for perfection or a predetermined end product.

Art journaling puts the focus on the process of exploration, rather than the product. It can be both art and journal writing. It can be used as a diary and a sketchbook all combined in one spot. Art journaling is freeing, playful and joyful—if the focus is on the experience rather than the end result of perfect pages. Art journaling can also be a place to work through challenges. The writing you add might be purely decorative but it may also be quite personal and cathartic. I have used the practice for both.

Art journaling is a gift to yourself. It is wrapped in a comfort quilt that whispers, "It is ok to start where you are this moment." There is no need for laborious foundation classes, hours of anatomy or life drawing lessons or a year-long class in color theory. Art journaling is a way to capture the moment, the thoughts

"What if" is a bridge from the comfort zone to the creative zone

and the energy of this exquisite and unique time. For me, it is a way to examine the minutiae of life; it helps anchor me in the moment. It can also provide a lens for examining the big transitions and major changes that roll in with various life cycles.

There are different genres for art journaling, which allows for individual approaches. Some use a journal as a file cabinet or a place to store and record ideas and reference information. Some journals are used to record travels, while other journals focus on nature sketches. There are art journals that are like Crock-Pots: Every imaginable art material gets thrown on a page to see what happens as the layers and textures build. Art journals can be used to record transitions in our lives, or times of stuck-ness. Art journals can hold our joy, our questions, our pain and (best of all) our growth.

The important aspect to keep in mind when working in an art journal is that every part of this endeavor is intended to be personalized. From the size and shape of your journal, to the many art materials you may wish to try out, there are a million choices and each choice allows you to follow a whim and experiment. The exploration itself is what brings me the greatest satisfaction. Every time I play with a new pen or a trusty old set of watercolors I wonder, "what will happen if…"

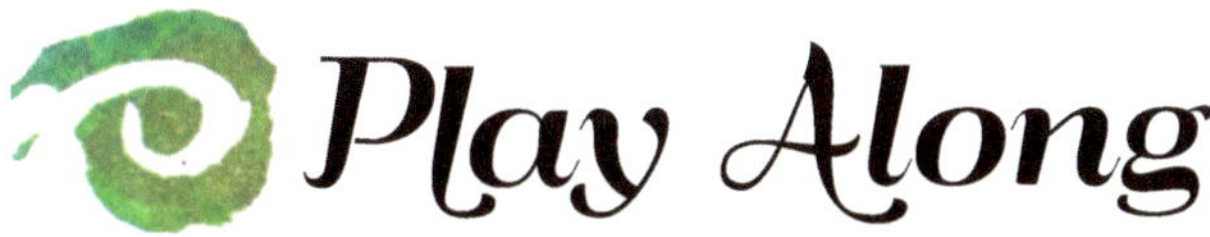 # Play Along

- **What if** I buy a different size journal? Will it influence the work that goes on each page?

- **What if** I find myself with only a ball-point pen and an old road map in the glove compartment of my car (and an extra 10 minutes)? What will happen if I use the map as my paper and the pen to sketch the birds on a post while I wait? What if I glue the sketch down on a page in my art journal?

- **What if** I am not happy with a page and I paint everything over with white paint or just keep adding color layers?

- **What if** I drop some of this color into that puddle of water?

- **What if** I rip this page then glue it over there?

- **What if** I give a friend a journal and some pens, and we work on our art journals together?

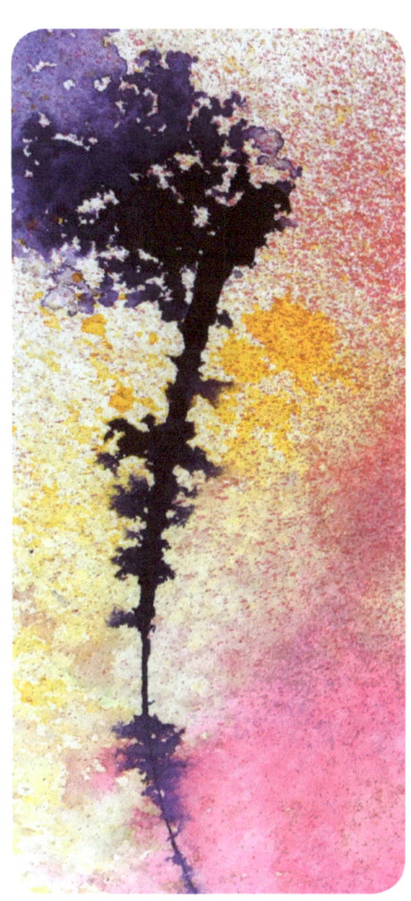

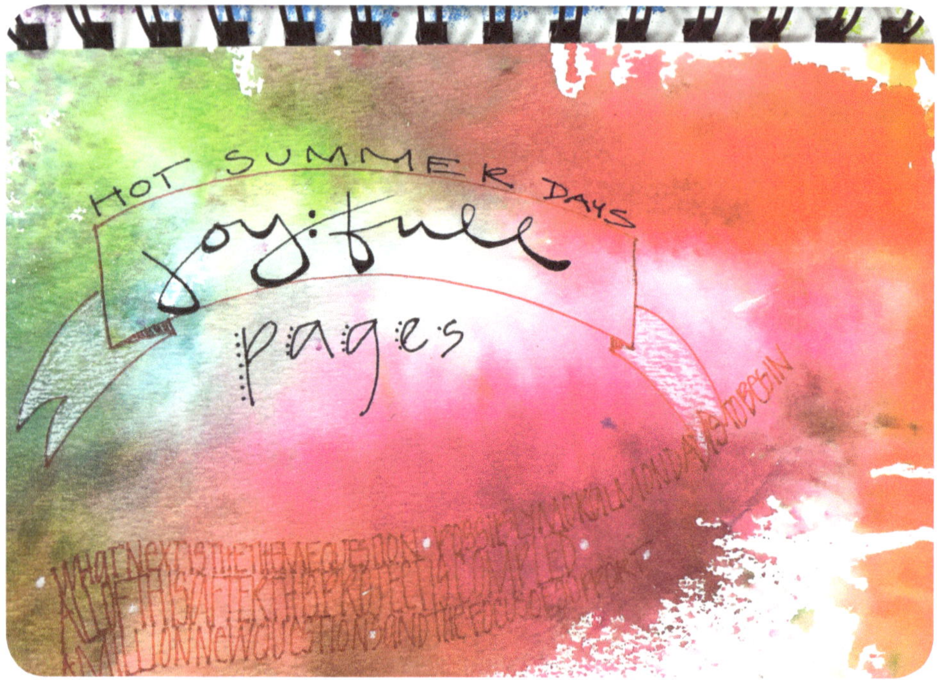

I add color to random pages in my journal, then layer over it with journaling that captures a moment or season in my life.

The simple "what if" question is key to art journaling. It creates an adventurous mindset and can crash through the barriers that keep us from actually doing something on a page. "What if" is a bridge from the comfort zone to the creative zone, from the predictable to delightful surprises, from an academic approach to art creation to the wide-open, inviting world of art journaling.

I am excited and honored to share this process and present a few of my favorite, no-fail techniques in this book. We will explore the creative zone, shed expectations about producing perfect pages and find joy in playful techniques. Anyone can art journal! No experience necessary; just bring a few materials and a willingness to step away from perfection. Your creative zone will expand as the pages fill. It will be a delightful ride together.

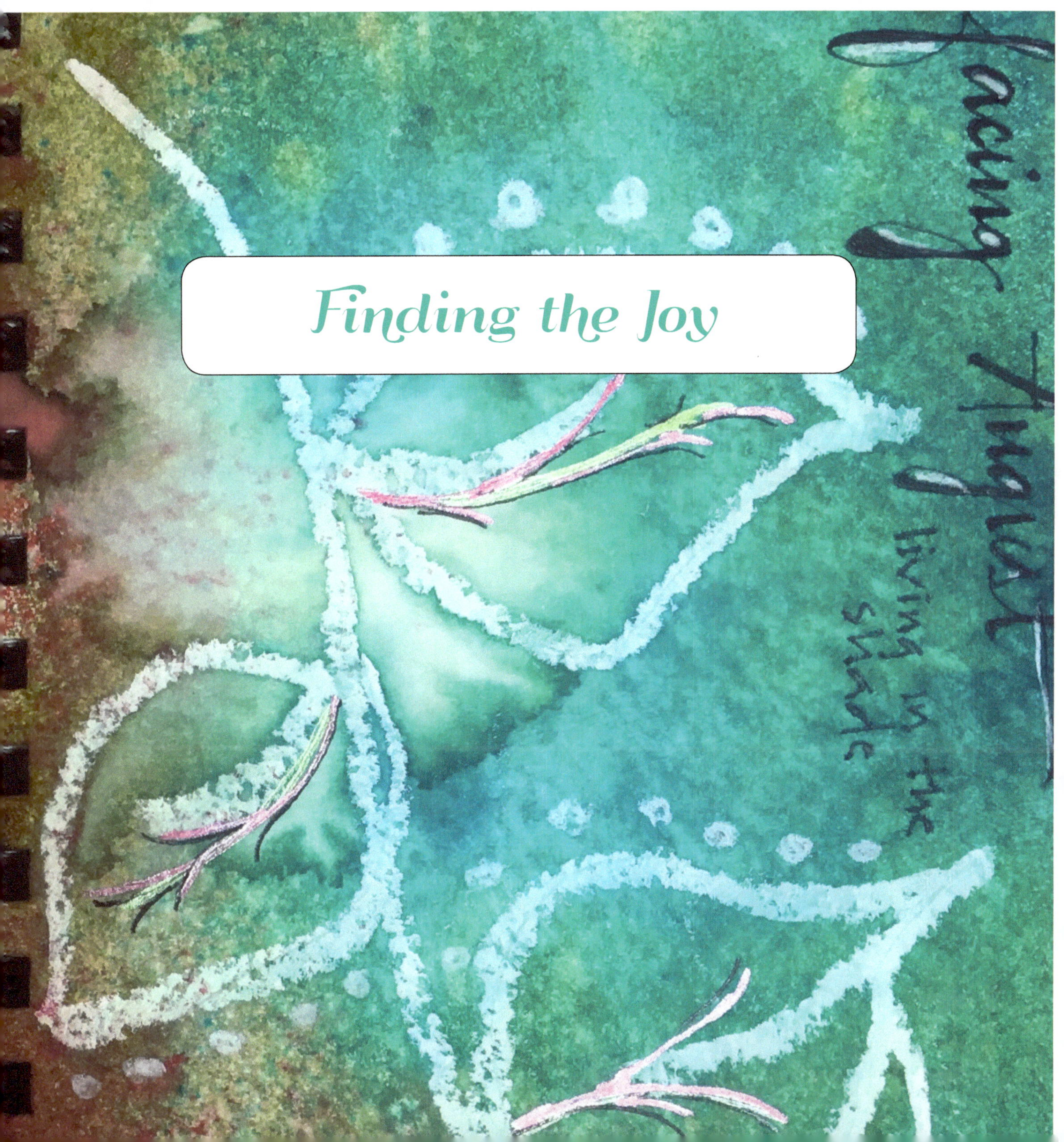

Finding the Joy

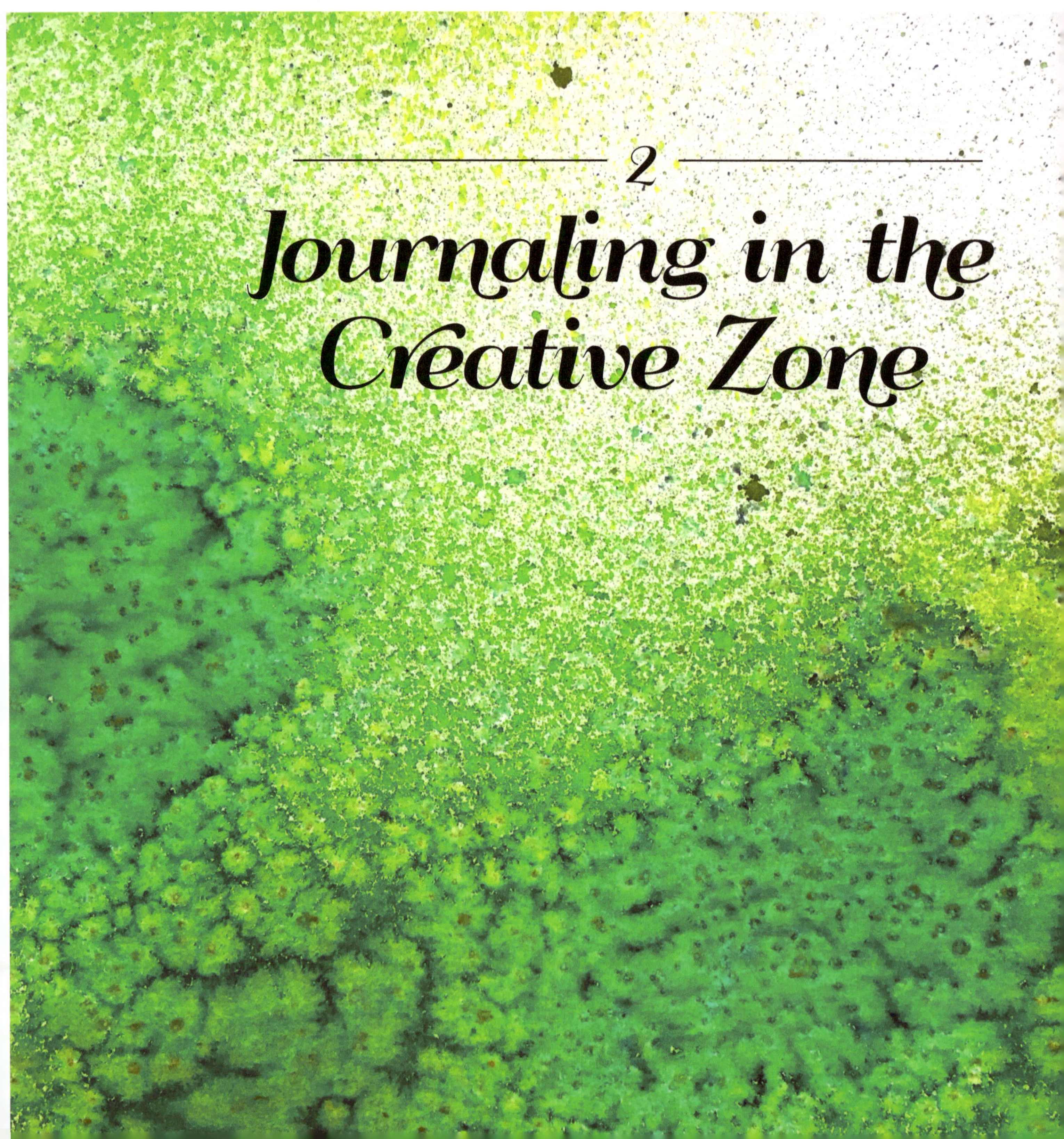

Journaling in the Creative Zone

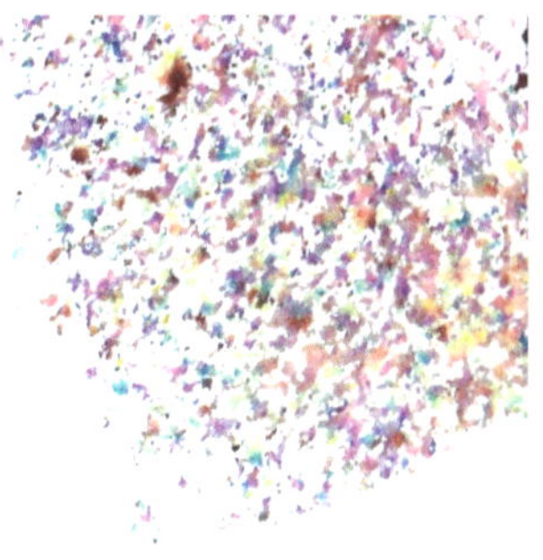

The term "getting in the zone" became popular based on the extensive research and writing of psychologist Mihaly Csikszentmihalyi. When Csikszentmihalyi published his book on flow in 1990, the concept of getting in the zone, or being in the flow, was not new. Ancient religions and philosophers long ago addressed the notion of time standing still and higher levels of consciousness, but he presented his research as a way to understand the possibilities of creativity in modern life and across all disciplines.

I loved discovering his research when I was in grad school a million years ago and still lean on his definition of flow: being in a mental space where skill meets concentration. It is where the task at hand is just rigorous enough to pull in our focus, and our skill level allows us to meet the challenge without being bored or so baffled that we lose interest and give up. The creative zone may be described as the experience when time stands still and daily concerns drop away for a little bit, leaving room for a mindset of "what if?"

I use the phrase creative zone interchangeably with flow. I like the visual images both phrases conjure. When was the last time you were in the creative zone? What were you concentrating on so thoroughly that time seemed to stand still?

Finding our way into the creative zone has a calming effect. By putting our attention on the possibilities and exploring luscious art materials, we can rise above the mundane aspects of our day and get a mental break from the doldrums or the stresses while engaging in a stimulating adventure of creation. If I am in a space of discomfort, with fear and sadness in my world, then my art journal can become a healing place as I work through those challenges. Other times, the journal pages capture joy in both mundane and special moments, reminding me to reside in gratitude and growth.

I acknowledge a slight contradiction at this point. Mindfulness is a pathway to examining our inner landscape; art journaling is a perfect place to record the process of a mindful examination of our world. Clarity and balance can unfold and our creative zone can include journal writing about who we are in this moment. But wait: Getting in the flow can also mean suspending linear, rational thought. Just moving, just painting, just staying in the "what if" place. This, too, is a function of art journaling. I consider this contradiction of thoughtful, deliberate writing versus wild abandonment with the art techniques an indication of the metaphoric "layers" that art journaling offers, and an open invitation to try it all and find what best fits your unique life.

This book includes journal prompts designed to help guide or direct some personal writing for your journal pages. You might want to explore the prompts and write on top of the art technique that was presented or you might be motivated to first write a response to the prompt on a blank page in your journal and wait for inspiration to add a second layer of color on top of your writing. You may not wish to write at all.

Explore, experiment, be open to the possibilities. You will find your own bridges into the creative zone.

Art Journaling and the Zone

My first career was as a public high school art teacher, my second career found me teaching creative expression at the university level and my current chapter allows me the opportunity to teach adults in various workshops in my hometown and around the country. I am in awe of the gentle yet profound experiences that mixed media art journaling has offered to my students at all levels.

My high school art students loved the freedom to explore and experiment in their mixed media journal pages. These were not traditional sketchbooks where there was a clear goal of developing drawing and observation skills. Instead, these books became incredibly personal places for capturing a moment, a thought, a feeling—through a variety of materials and with no rules except that pages needed to be filled.

My college students were not art majors. They were fulfilling a school-wide requirement to take a creative expression class. These busy, stressed students entered my class with an assumption that it was going to

explore
experiment

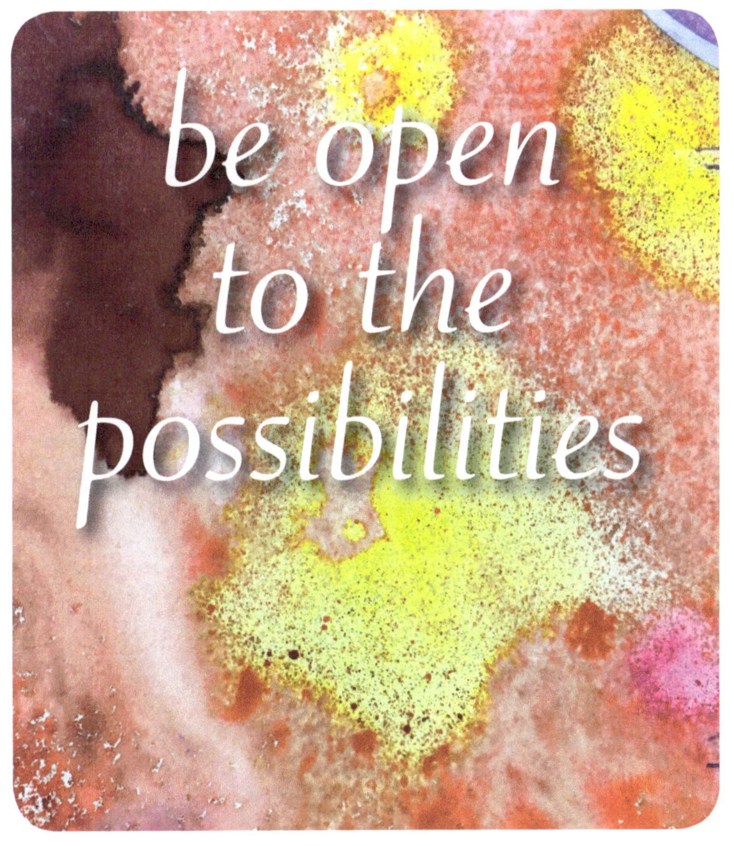

be either ridiculously easy or ridiculously challenging to a non-art person. It was a joy to witness students enter their zone; where their skill level met the challenge of the daily journal prompt and art technique. Students at this level were surprised at how personally fulfilling and meaningful the mixed media approach became, and I have kept in touch with students who have shared that over the years of moving into very challenging careers they kept their balance through journaling.

Adults who come to an introduction to art journaling class always leave saying the four or five hours flew by. For many, this approach offers a reminder that there is a creative side they had either long forgotten or never recognized. Some of my students choose an art journaling class as a way to reconnect with an inner voice. Others come for no reason other than it is something fun to do with a friend. Once a student experiences the time-less, deep concentration and pure joy that comes when something random turns into something beautiful, an art journaler is born. What a privilege to witness!

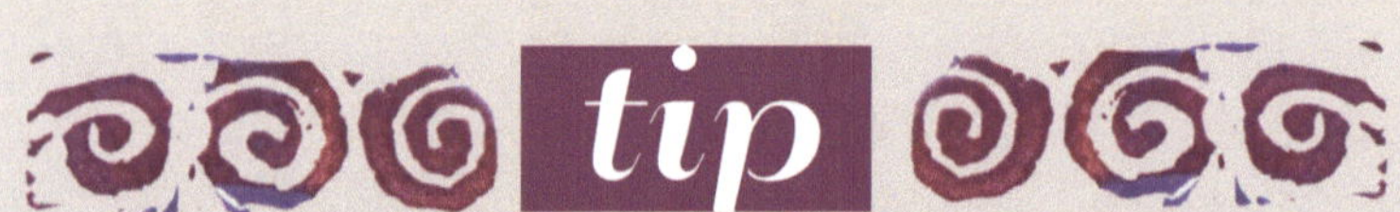

Having your materials handy
+ carving out a little time
+ mustering up a bit of confidence
= the start of an art journal practice that will lead you
into joyful pages and the creative zone!

Art journals are places to capture

a moment,

a thought,

a feeling.

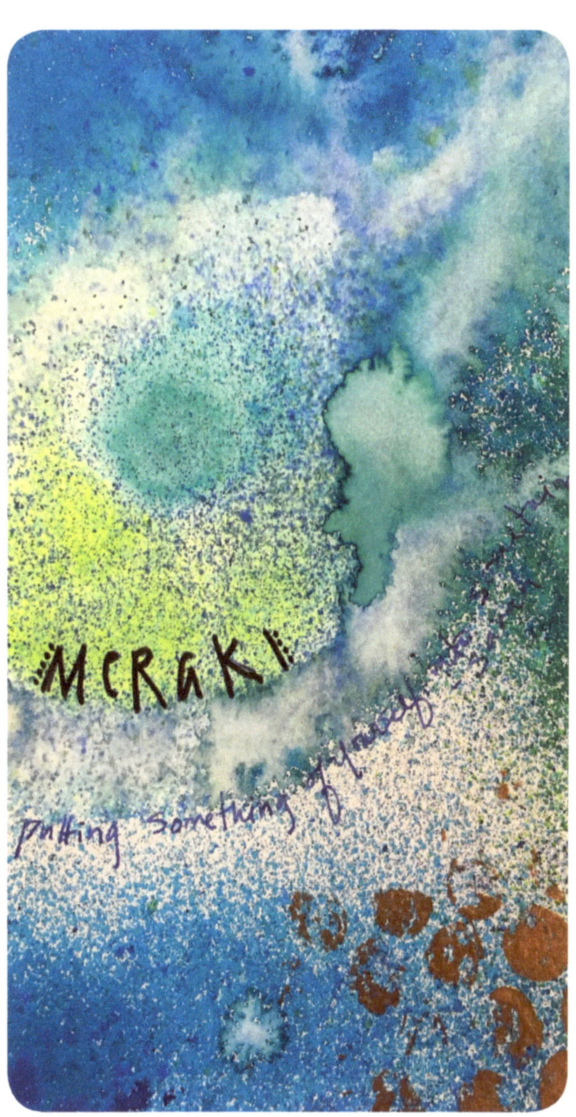

The art materials we use in this book are low-cost and accessible for all ability levels. They will provide delightful results that are unique to each person. Playing with the techniques will engage you and help create that zone where time might stand still and you emerge from the lesson feeling refreshed.

Along with the materials and techniques, I offer journal writing prompts to round out the experience. Some students find journal prompts help to develop interesting layers (of text or ideas) on the pages, while others might find the prompts limiting. I encourage you to pick and choose; work with the best and leave the rest. There are no rules. If the journal prompts resonate, then I invite you to explore them for a deeper, personal experience. If they act as roadblocks, then jump on over and remember that there are no rules. You get to choose how to play and explore.

The basic materials are discussed in the next chapter. You can choose which technique to explore, then gather your supplies as you go or you can grab everything at once and be ready to play with the different processes as the mood strikes. Regardless of how you approach the material list, I suggest taking some time to consider how you will store your supplies so they are accessible and easy to keep organized. I keep my materials in clear plastic bins when possible so I can see where things are hanging out and they are easy to grab. One of the quickest ways to de-rail joyful art journaling is to let your busy schedule make it hard to find time to get going. If you keep your supplies in an easy-to-access box, the whole process of opening your book and giving it some love will be simplified.

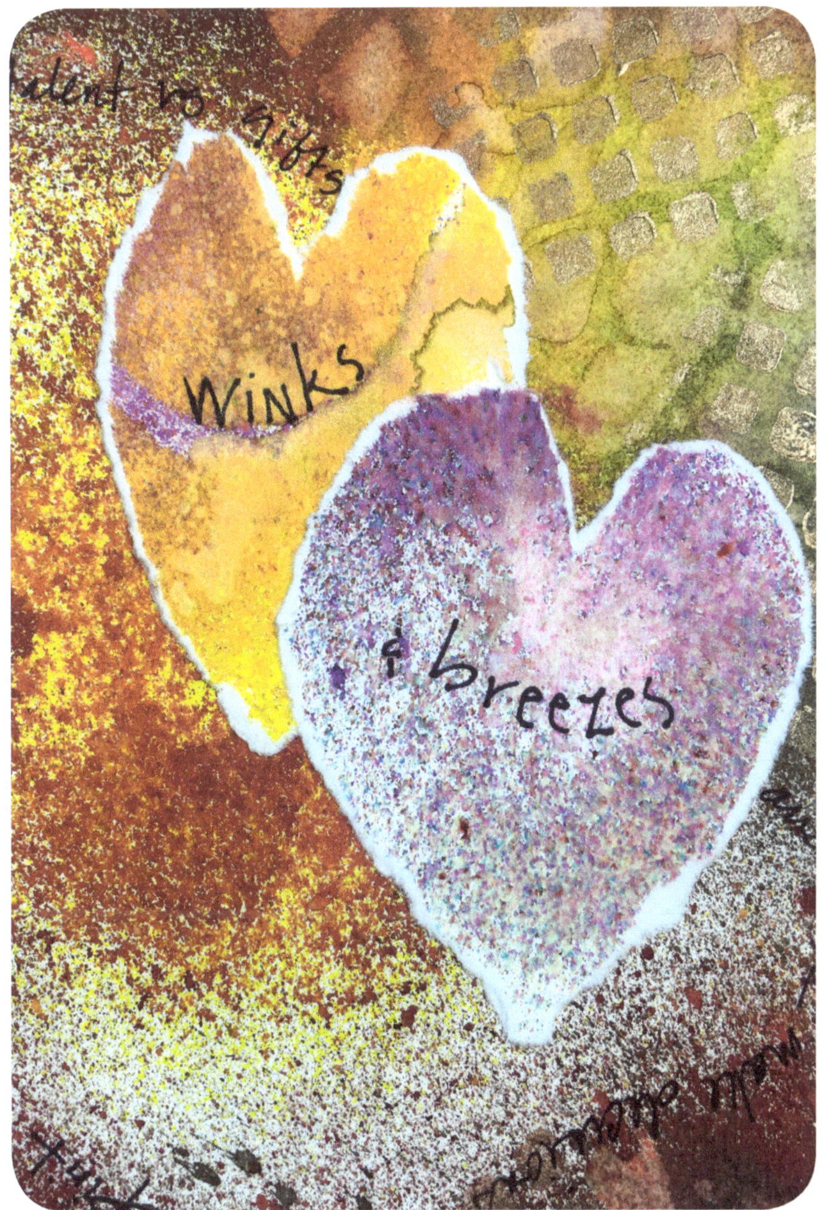

A bit of journaling on a colorful background helps me capture a fleeting moment on the page.

3
Supplies for the Journey

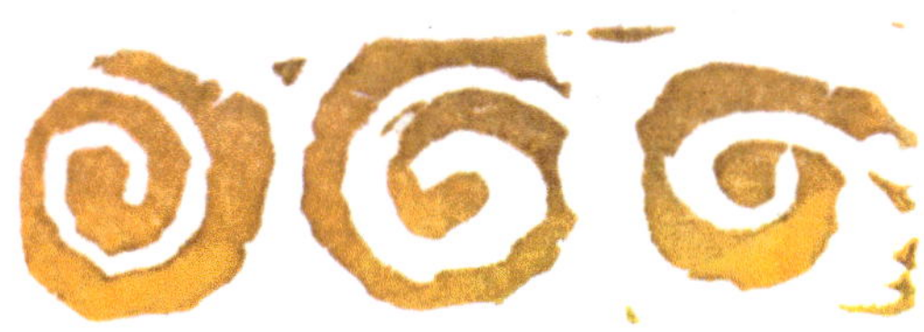

To find your zone and get started playing with your journal pages you don't need to amass a studio full of supplies. Keep it simple and manageable; the materials we will work with can be used in a wide variety of ways.

The supply list may appear to be long, but you can choose a technique or two to start with and only buy a few items at a time. Some students prefer to gather everything at once so they are ready to go as they explore each chapter.

The "adventure" part of this process lies in discovering what else you can do with the inks, chalks and pens as you find your own favorites and explore your unique expression on each page.

Feel free to substitute materials you might already have in your home. The most important item will be the paper you work on. If you use inexpensive paper, then the spray inks and crayon resist techniques will not be satisfying. Rubber stamps work well on pretty much any surface. If you are only buying one or two items, I encourage you to invest in a blank art journal book with good quality paper.

An art journal

This is basically a sketchbook (blank paper) with heavier weight, good quality paper. I recommend either "mixed media" or watercolor paper (90 lb), in a 5½-by-8-inch size book or something similar.

I like Aquabee and Strathmore journals that come with either mixed media or watercolor paper. Both of these brands have books with coil bindings that allow the book to lay flat when open. They also both have hard covers, which will protect your pages and make the books stand up to some traveling.

Practice paper

In addition to your art journal, I suggest getting a pad of larger paper to use for practice, such as a Canson XL Mixed Media Pad (9 by 12 or 11 by 14 inches) or any brand of 90 lb watercolor paper.

We will practice techniques described in chapters 4 and 5 on this paper then cut up the paper for use in later chapters. I find that students are most comfortable trying wild, new techniques on practice paper first, then working on their journal pages directly.

Pens

I like the Sakura Micron pens with very fine tips; I use the 005 or 02 for most of my work. They are permanent and waterproof. Buy a few since the tiny tips wear out easily.

We will also work with a water-reactive pen called a Tombow Dual Brush marker.

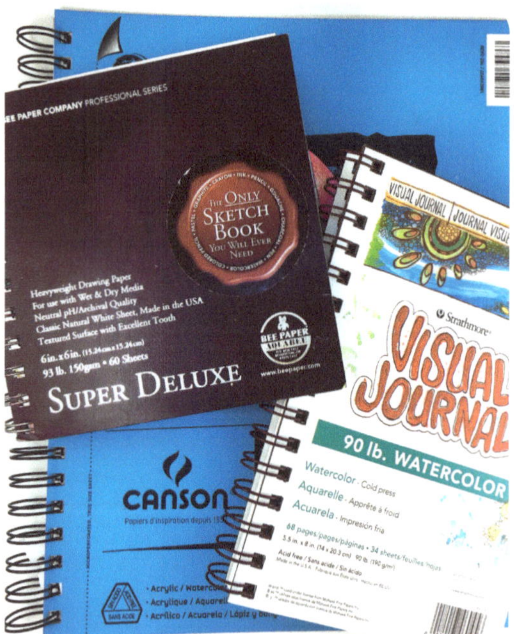

Choose a journal with good-quality paper to make the most of the Joyful Pages techniques.

Water-reactive means that the ink will move, blend and bleed when water is applied to the mark on the page. Tombows come in a wide variety of yummy colors but you really only need one or two for our explorations.

A Pigma Brush pen (by Sakura) is something you will enjoy when we talk about adding text to our pages. This pen has permanent ink and won't change if water touches the mark, and the easy-to-control brush gives a lovely thick and thin line.

Glue stick

I use a glue stick as my go-to adhesive for almost everything in my art journals. Inexpensive glue sticks are all you need: The brand is not as important as the application process.

India ink

I love the personality of India inks; they are fun and highly pigmented with great colors. India ink uses a type of varnish as a binder. This varnish gives the product the versatility and stability that is different from other inks (like acrylic ink). The varnish allows the ink to dry with a slightly shiny or harder surface, rendering the color permanent on your page. However, while the ink is wet or in the stages of drying it will react to water by bleeding, blooming or spreading around the page. Some of the movement of ink and water can be controlled, some is just a magical dance that is terrific fun to watch.

My preferred brand is Dr. Ph. Martin's Bombay Inks as they come in fabulous colors and are the least expensive.

Most artists will dip an ink pen into the ink and draw; I prefer to drip and spray the inks in a freer, more intuitive manner as described in chapter 4. I suggest you start off purchasing only two different colors that call your name. These colors should work well together, so stay with either two warm colors

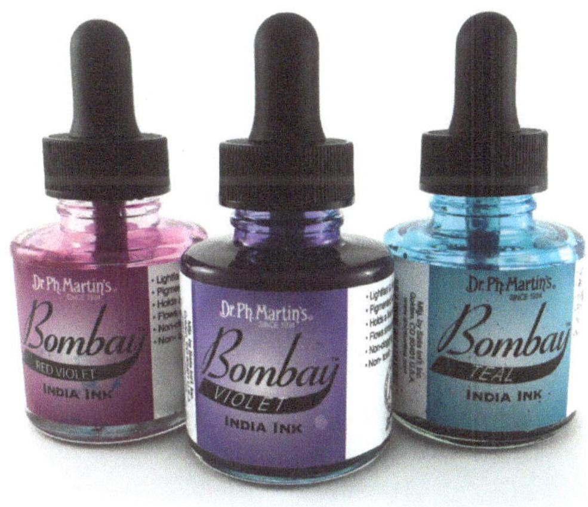

You'll fall in love with the rich colors and fluidity of India ink. Start by choosing just a few colors you love.

or two cool colors, such as blue and purple, purple and magenta, red and orange, etc.

India inks will stain your skin for days and your clothes permanently, so be sure to protect your work surface and wear nitrile gloves.

Dylusions spray inks

These inks first showed up in the scrapbook world but quickly expanded to be used by many art journalers. There are 18 colors in the full line; all are delicious and highly pigmented so the colors are rich and intense. These inks don't ever become permanent so working with them can be interesting. The pigments can transfer to your skin even after a page has been drying for several days. Good news: This allows you to add water (on a wet paint brush) to bleed and blend areas of the ink many days after you initially sprayed the product on your page. Bad news: They are not permanent so you have to be aware that the colors will bleed if you add anything wet on top at any time down the road. These inks will also stain your skin, so be sure to read about nitrile gloves and use them.

The differences between the Dylusions ink and India inks should be kept in mind: The India inks will clog the pump spray a bit faster because of the larger particles of varnish used in the formula, but when they are dry they are permanent. When dry, the colors won't lift onto your fingers even if they get damp.

The Dylusions come in many colors, the pumps might clog (not as much as the India inks), but they will lift off the paper and continue to stain your hands as you work with these pages over a few days. They will also bleed when any moisture comes in contact with the page, which is actually a characteristic I love.

I suggest the following colors for a "beginner set" of Dylusions, there is no need to purchase all 18 until you know you will love and use them.

Lemon Zest
Postbox Red
London Blue
Crushed Grape
Vibrant Turquoise

You may notice that I listed the three primary colors (red, blue and yellow), plus two secondary colors (purple and a turquoise green). To achieve additional colors, you can easily mix these five in various combinations just as you might mix watercolors or any other paint.

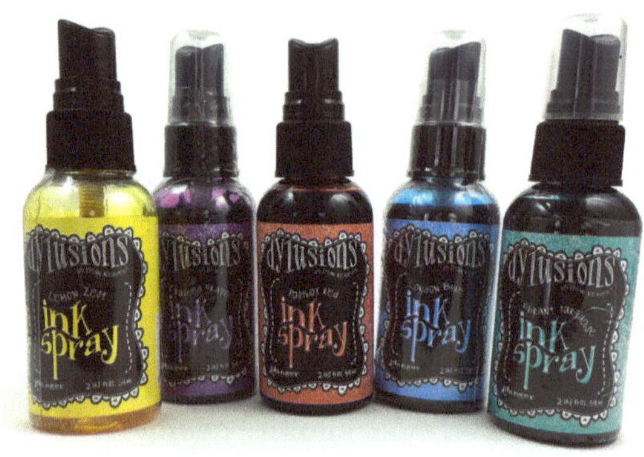

Spray inks from Dylusions offer art journalers intriguing options for adding color to a page.

Nitrile gloves

I have been teaching at the Art Student League of Denver for over 15 years. The organization asked a team of medical professionals to observe and study the way artists typically use various materials (ranging from oil paints to watercolors to pencils and inks). After an extensive study, a safe art practice was advised and I share it with all of my students: It is preferable to keep all pigments off of the skin.

Not complicated. These pigments can be India inks, Dylusion inks, watercolor paint, rubber stamp ink, chalk pastels, acrylic paints... anything that has color in it.

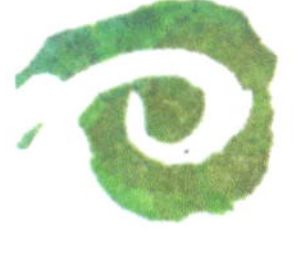

The Foolproof Guide to Using Glue Sticks

1. Work on a recycled catalog (or some junk mail) where the page is slightly bigger than the item you are gluing. This catalog page or scrap paper will catch stray glue swipes and is called the "waste paper." It can be recycled after use.

2. Set your item to be glued face down on the waste paper.

3. Apply glue to the entire back surface, being careful to move your glue stick off all the edges onto the waste paper. This is the most important step! Double check that every surface is covered in the glue. (You might like to use glue that goes on purple before drying clear, so you can see exactly where you have applied the glue.)

4. Flip your item over and set it where you'd like on your journal page, then burnish (or rub) the entire area so every surface makes contact with the page you are gluing to. By rubbing the entire surface, you will eliminate any air bubbles that can create pockets allowing the glue to dry out. If you can avoid air pockets, your glue will behave nicely, keeping your item in the proper place for a very long time.

5. Turn to a new page in your waste paper catalog or grab a new piece of scrap paper to use when applying glue to your next item.

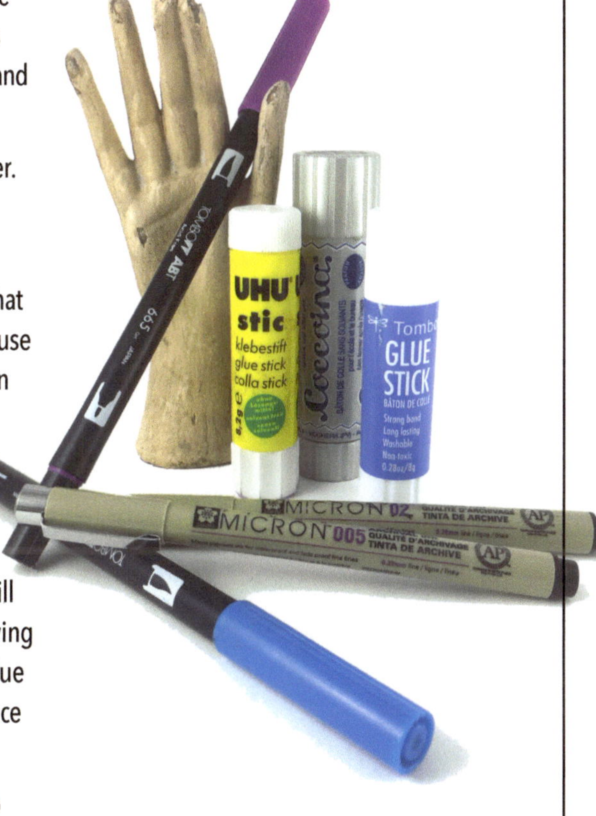

So, the first purchase for my students is a box of nitrile gloves, which are disposable (but can be rinsed off and re-used for a long time). Nitrile gloves may be found in most drug stores and pharmacy aisles as well as in the big box home improvement stores. I suggest that you wear them when working with any of the inks. They are great for anything messy. Students have asked about skin barrier creams that are on the market, but the nitrile gloves make the best barrier without exposing your skin to additional chemicals that are found in the hand lotions.

For your safety, use nitrile gloves to keep paint, chalk or ink pigments off your skin.

Small pump spray bottles

You can use a single bottle for both water and ink if you wash it between uses, or work with two separate bottles. Both art and craft stores carry small spray bottles. Larger pharmacies often sell spray bottles in their travel container section. I like to up-cycle empty cosmetic pump spray bottles.

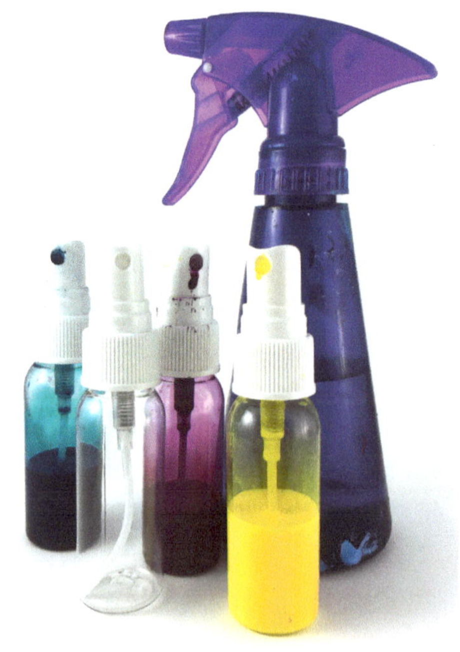

Large spray bottles and mini pump sprayers make mixing and applying ink easy and fun.

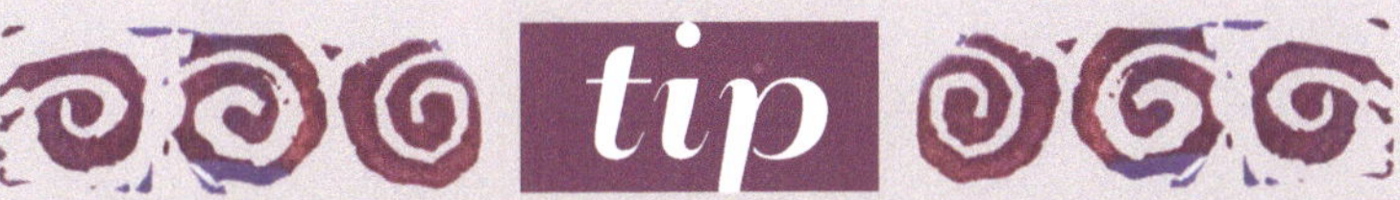

You'll see lots of photos on social media and video tutorial sites of painted hands, making it look like great fun to jump right in with your fingers. I love the joy and fun captured in those images, but I cringe a little bit at the message. My suggestion is to be safe and keep the pigments off your skin. Plus, it is an easier cleanup all around to just remove and dispose of the gloves.

Chalk pastels

In general, chalk pastels are not a great journal medium because they can get very messy and will smudge easily. In chapter 6, I describe a unique application process that allows us to use chalk pastels in our art journal without concern about smudging. The pastels I like to work with are from Faber-Castell (24 half sticks in a set) but any chalk pastel will work. It is best if they have the labels removed from the individual sticks as you will not be picking them up with your fingers for the application. Please be sure not

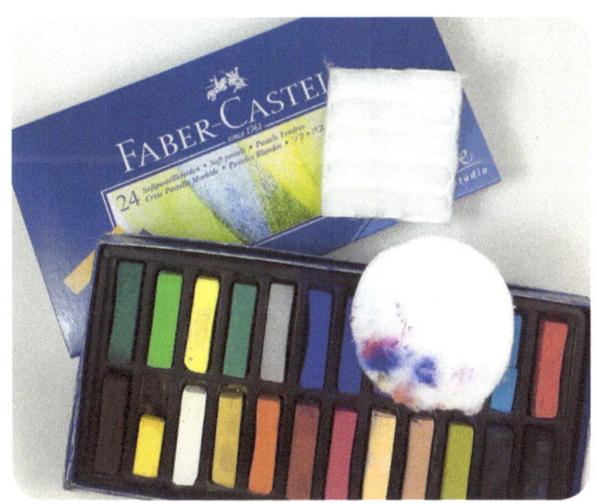

Use cotton rounds or squares for a no-mess way to apply chalk pastels to your art journal pages.

to use oil pastels for this process as they will not work. Pastels will be applied with cotton rounds (or squares) found in the cosmetics area of your drug or grocery store.

White gesso

White gesso (pronounced jeh-sew) is a white acrylic paint with a little plaster mixed in. It's most often used to prepare canvas for oil or acrylic painting, but mixed media artists turn to gesso for a variety of techniques beyond the original intent. Art journalers use gesso on their pages to achieve different effects. I often apply gesso as a top coat and as a recovery tool or a "reset button" when I have a page that is not working out the way I had hoped and the layers are getting a bit out of hand.

You can paint white gesso on top of any of the materials we will use. It will dry with a slight transparency so you can still see a hint of what is below under a dreamy, cloudy layer of the gesso. This is an optional material to have on hand.

You only need a small container (or tube) of gesso and any brand will work. Since this is an acrylic product, it will clean up with water while wet, but once it has dried it will be permanent. Protect your clothes and wash

the brush out as soon as you are finished painting an area.

Commercial stencils

Here is another rabbit hole to fall into: The world of commercial stencils has exploded. Stencils are great for art journaling because they are flat, made of strong plastic and come in a huge variety of patterns. I suggest you

Search your house inside and out for items that will work as stencils or masks.

purchase a few that you love; patterns and designs will be more versatile than stencils with specific imagery or phrases.

Look for stencils online or in the scrapbook department of craft stores as well as some art supply stores (near the air brush supplies). They generally come in two sizes. I suggest the smaller size (6 by 6 inches) since it will likely fit more easily on your journal page. I like The Crafters Workshop or Stencil Girl line because they offer many pattern and texture stencils.

A word about terminology: There is a difference between a "stencil" and a "mask" although you don't see the term mask used too often in various mixed media publications. A mask is a positive shape, or an item like a feather, which is put on the page and spray is applied over it. When you lift the mask after applying paint you are left with a

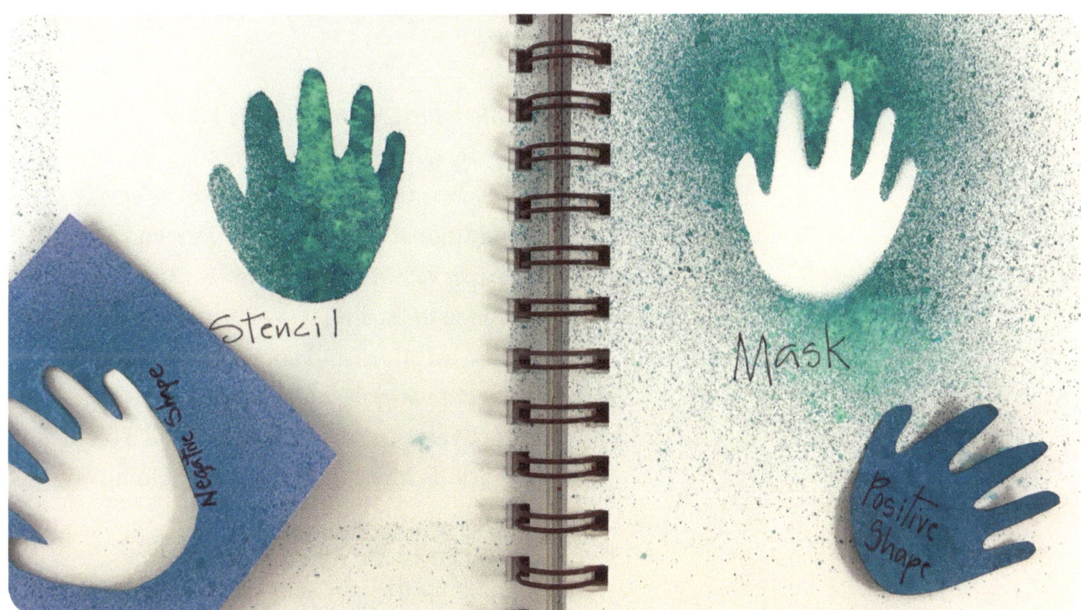

A stencil is a negative shape that leaves a positive shape behind on a page. A mask is a positive shape that leaves a negative space behind when sprayed over with paint or ink.

"negative" shape, or a silhouette of the object. A stencil is the opposite; you start with a shape cut out of a sheet of plastic (or stiff paper). When you spray over that open shape or area then lift the stencil, an image appears. With a stencil you go from a negative shape to a positive shape; a mask is the opposite.

Vintage book pages

We will look at how text can be used to add depth, meaning or just graphic design to a journal page. A quick and satisfying way to get text on a page is to glue down some discarded text from a book that has reached the end of its life (or you can photocopy a page from a book that you would prefer not to cut up). I suggest working with a vintage book that really is not too vintage; avoid yellow or brittle pages, as these won't glue well. Also, it is best to avoid text on glossy paper (as in old textbooks) as this paper does not accept paint or ink well and will limit what layers you can add to the page.

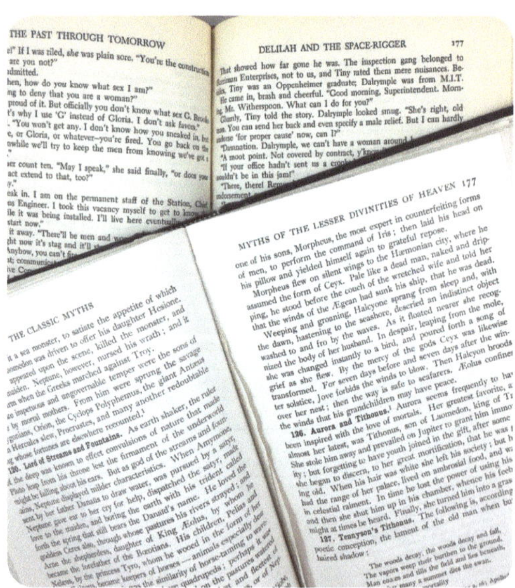

Pages torn (or photocopied) from vintage or discarded books are perfect for adding layers and interest.

Masking tape and washi tape

Tape helps create interactive elements in art journaling and can also be used as an additional decorative component on your page. Washi tape (a name for thin, paper tape made in Japan) is now found in most craft and art stores and comes in a million different patterns. Sometimes the sticky side is not very sticky, so it helps to add a bit of glue stick if you find that it is not holding onto the page as you hoped.

We will use the circle shape on the inside of the roll of masking tape for a few different techniques. I love black masking tape, but any color or brand will work.

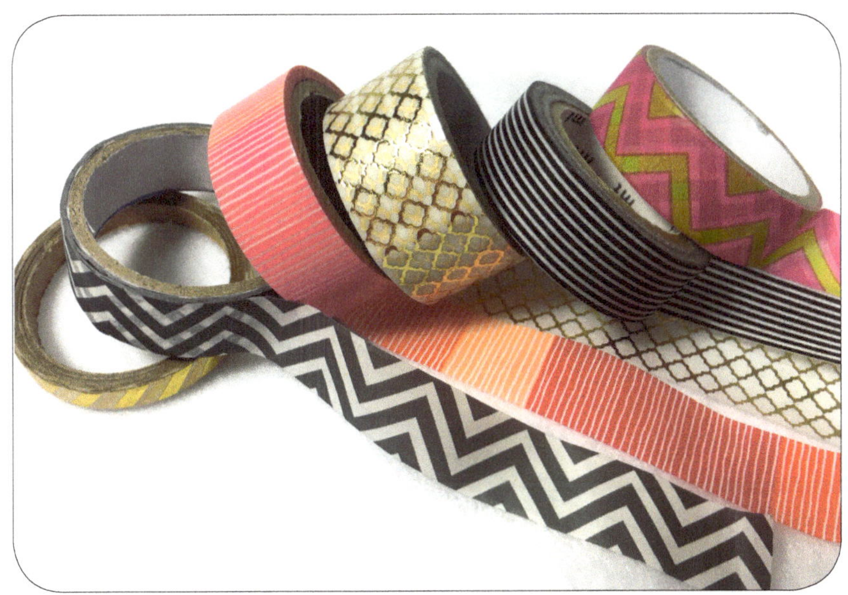

Patterned washi tape as well as plain and colored masking tape (like the black tape shown below) can be used for decoration or for holding items in place on your journal pages.

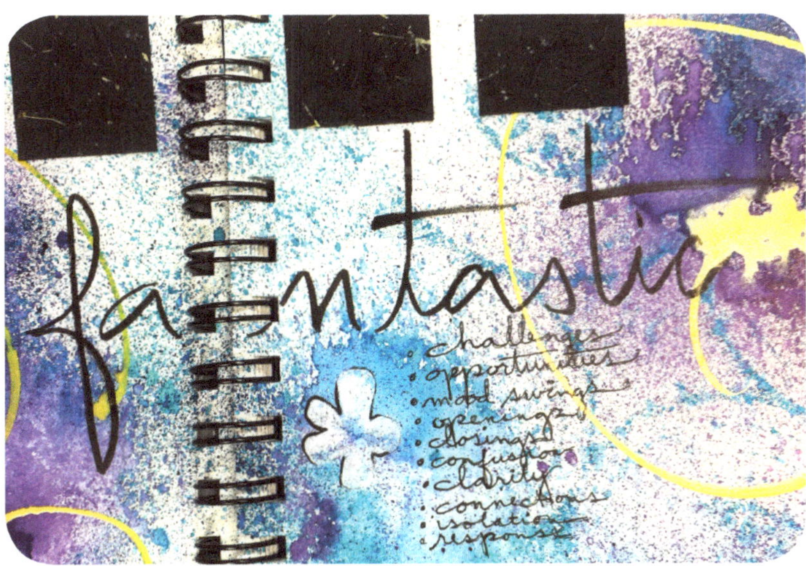

Other basic materials to gather:

Plastic cloth to cover your work surface (check out the white plastic tablecloths in the party section of dollar stores)

Apron

Paper towels (you will use a lot of these with our wet techniques)

Wax paper to protect your journal pages

Push pin to poke a hole through the papers (you can use a book awl if you have one)

Found objects to use as stencils and masks for spray painting

Decorative fasteners or brads, any size

Small, inexpensive paint brush

White cray pas oil pastel (this looks like a regular crayon but has a higher wax/oil content)

Table salt or kosher salt

Cotton rounds or squares (found in the cosmetics section of any pharmacy)

Pencil with an eraser

Index card

Scissors

Rubber stamps, preferably with patterns and designs, not specific images

Rubber stamp inkpad (either pigment ink, dye ink or Distress ink)

Cardstock tags (shipping tags are larger than the merchandise tags, either will work)

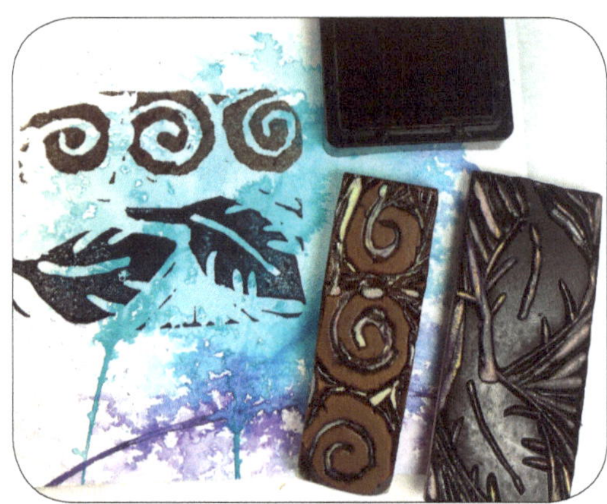

Commerical or hand-carved rubber stamps can be used to add texture to your journal pages.

Discarded catalogs, magazines or junk mail to use when applying glue stick

Plastic tubs to hold all your materials are key, because having your materials easy to find and store will make a huge difference in your art journal efforts

Layering

Now that you have considered the art materials we will explore, it is important to understand a key concept in art journaling, which will help clarify the crazy range of art materials we will be using.

Layering is a basic tool, but not a rule.

One of the appealing aspects to art jour-

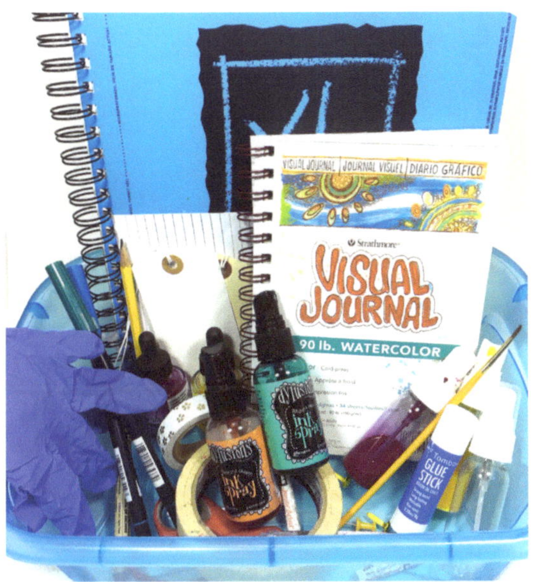

Don't waste precious creative energy searching for supplies: Corral all your essentials in a plastic bin or tub.

naling is working in layers on the page. It might help to think about pizza or cupcakes: When you imagine these yummy treats, you will likely see layers of goodness. You think of crust and sauce, cheese and toppings. You drool over cake with icing and sprinkles. Our senses are tickled when there are layers and texture—in the food world and in the art world alike.

On the other hand, since there are no rules, you are encouraged to experiment with pages in your journal that only have one layer, or a single visual element standing alone. You might find satisfaction in the variety as you explore your own unique voice. I encourage you to see how the layers feel, then try ignoring this concept to see what you like.

One nice advantage of taking the layered approach is to embrace the adage: "If you are not thrilled with a page just add a little more." (There is room for you in the More Is More Club.) Layers can also hide areas that are not giving you joy.

Another aspect of layering is that the order of the techniques really does not matter. I might write some thoughts on a page first, using my handwriting as the first layer. Then I will add some of the spray techniques (see chapters 4 and 5) over the handwriting. I might glue a little collage piece on top of everything, or I could create a page going in reverse order. I might glue something down, then spray over that, and then write a response to a journal prompt on top. Unlike so many art forms that require a step-by-step approach, art journaling with a variety of media is more about a dance of layers based on how you feel at the time you are working on a few pages.

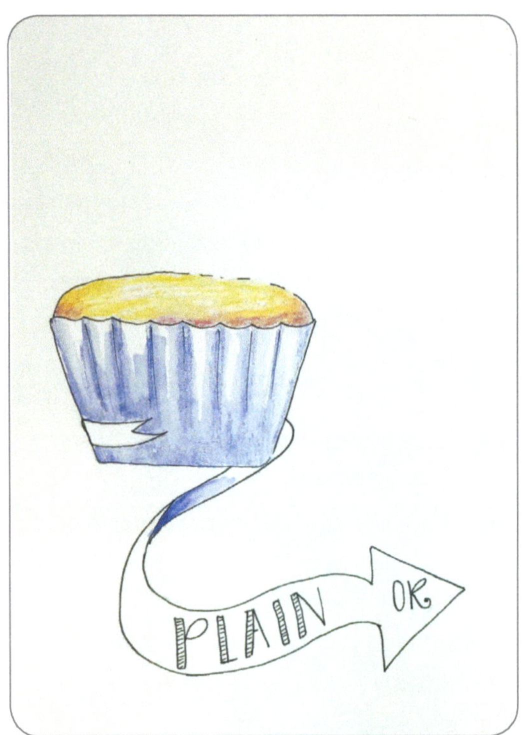
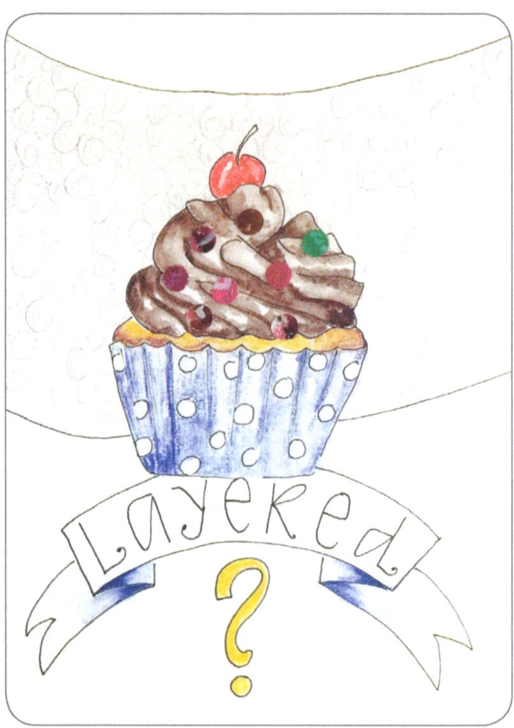

Do you prefer plain or layered? Try journal pages both ways to find out!

Embrace the "what if" mindset

The huge range of art materials we will play with in this book reflect the layered approach to art journaling and endless possibilities. Some materials will move when a wet medium is applied (these materials are called "water reactive"). Some materials are stable and permanent when dry. We can put one layer of wet ink on top of permanent pen marks, we can put pen marks on top of ink that has dried. We can do a little something on a

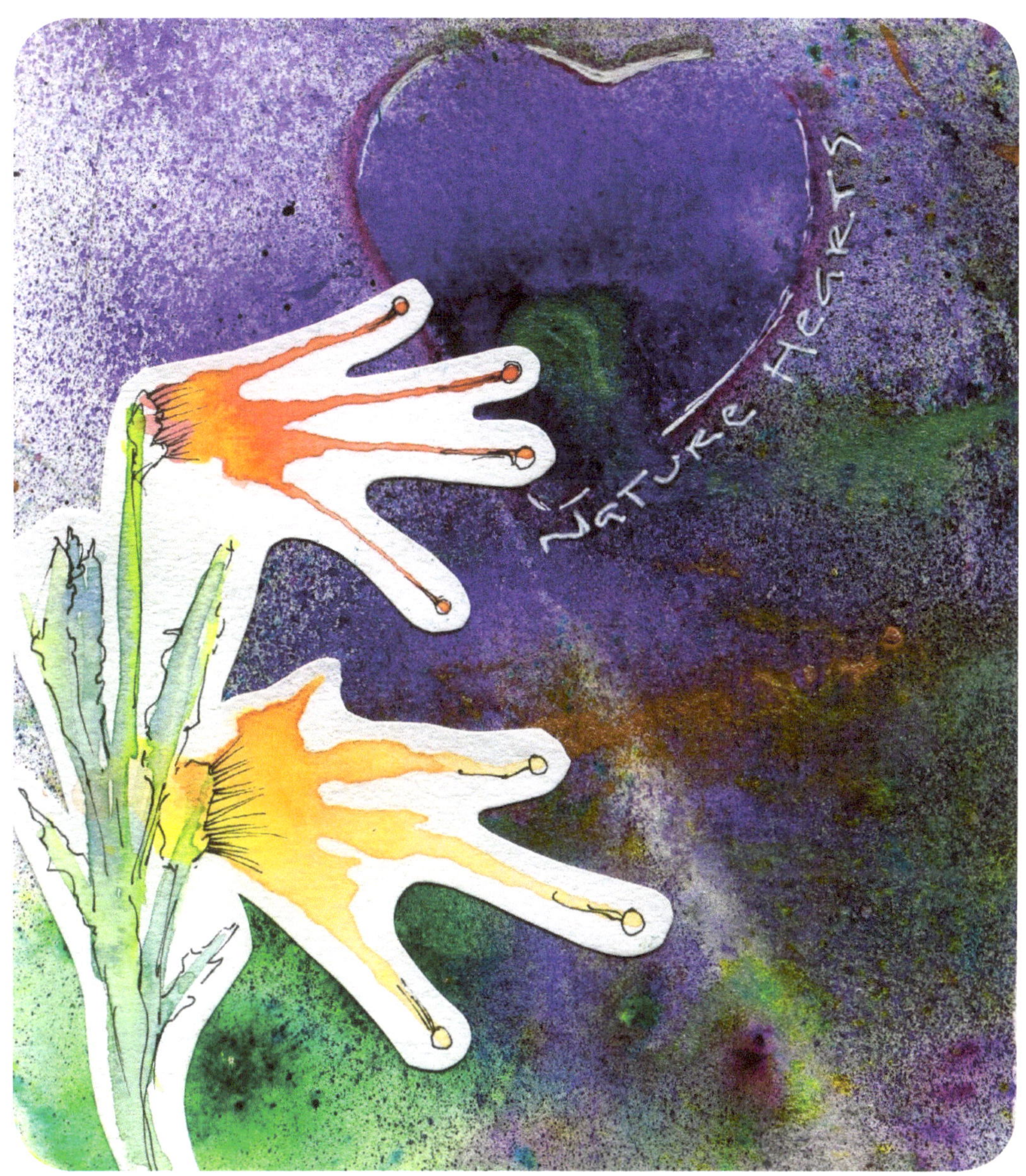

Ink blooms become flower blossoms that I collaged on top of an ink-sprayed background. I added text as a top layer.

page, then go back days or weeks later to add a splash of color or a border of rubber stamp ink. Traditional art materials, like oil paints, watercolor or clay, typically require a linear approach with one accepted way to work with the medium. As we find our flow and create joyful pages, we will throw out convention and focus more on building luscious layers.

Even as I offer instructions for techniques, I encourage you to question the directions, come up with your own applications and embrace the "what if" mindset.

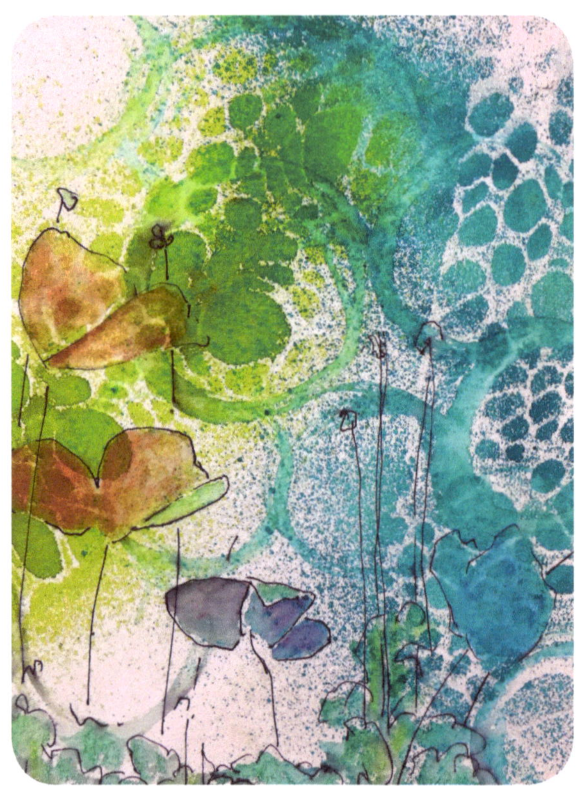

Doodles add another layer over stenciled designs and a sprayed-ink background.

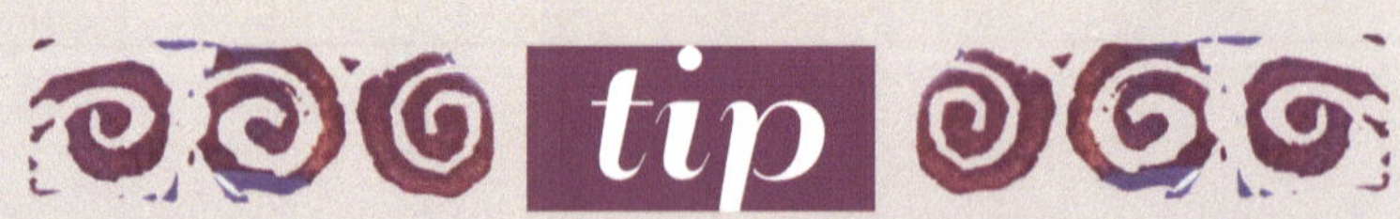

Invest in a blank art journal book with good quality paper.

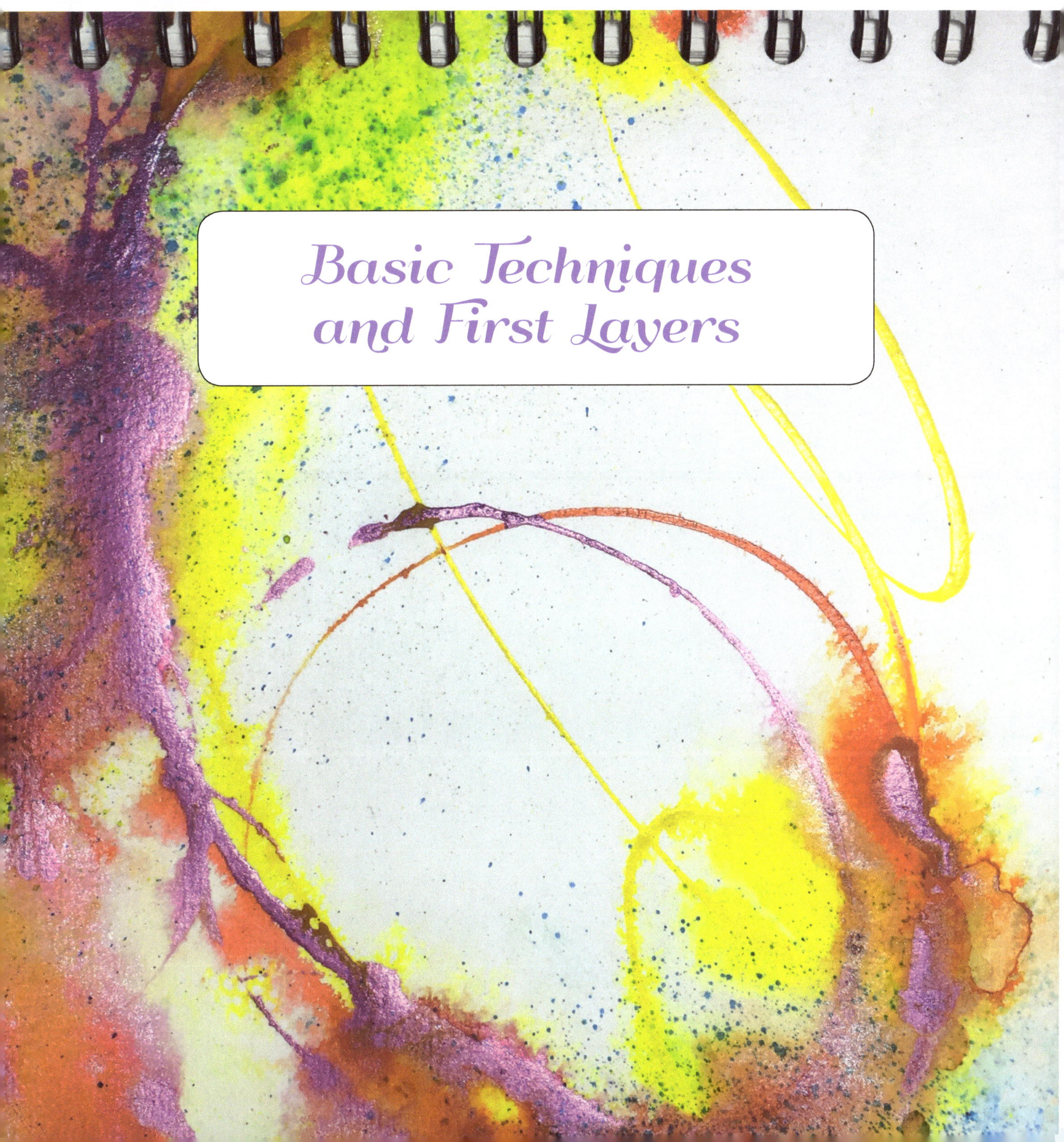

Basic Techniques
and First Layers

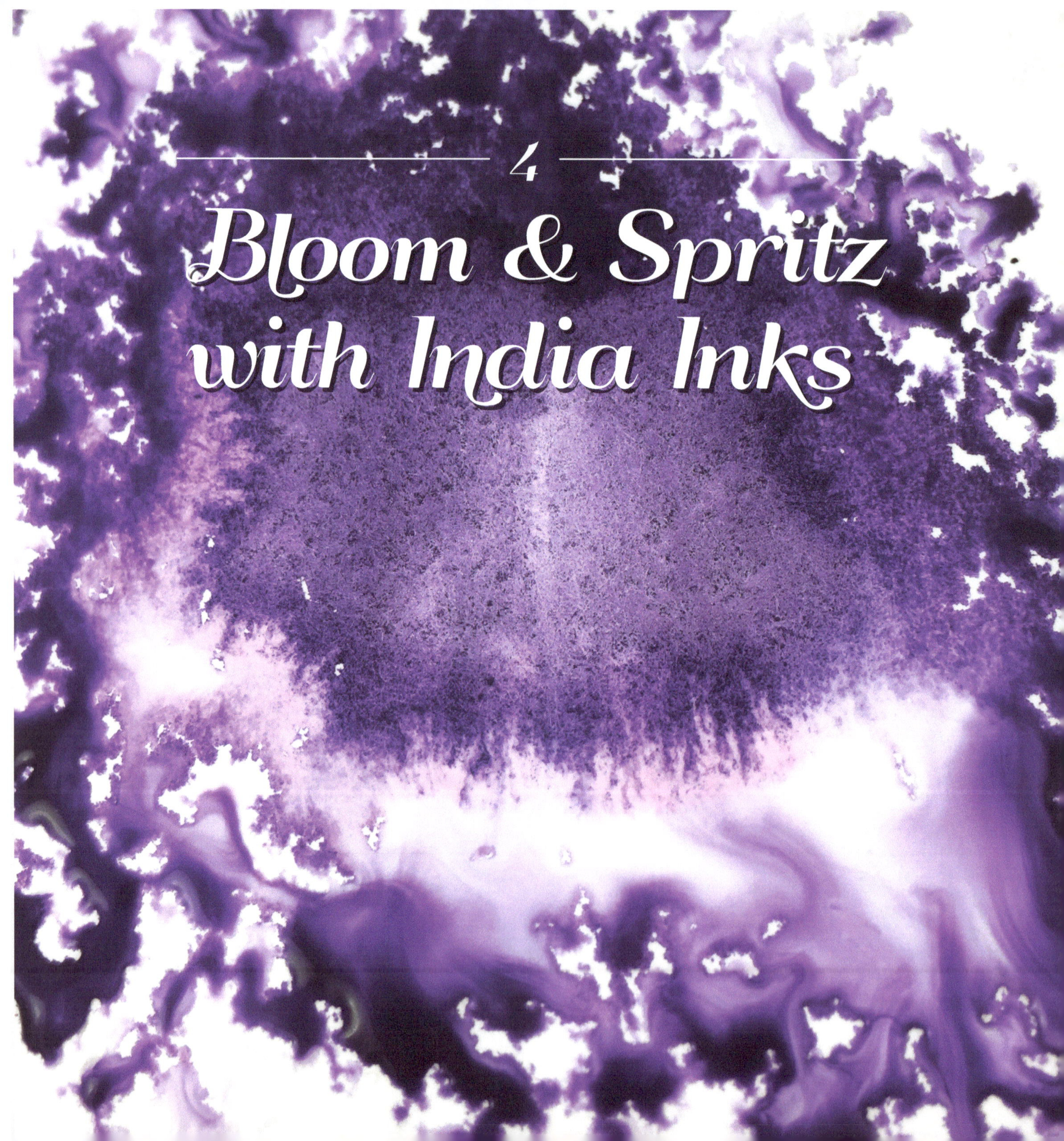

Bloom & Spritz with India Inks

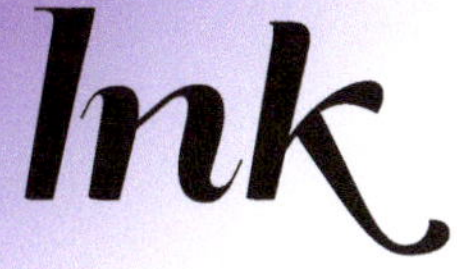 Ink

called India ink is a fairly common art material, most often used with dipping pens or paint brushes for application. We are going to get in the zone and play with India ink in a new way; one that will mesmerize and delight.

One unique quality of India ink is that when it dries it is permanent on the paper. No amount of water will move, bleed or blur the lines. But while it is still wet or damp, it can react to additional water in marvelous ways. It will dance, flow, bloom and seem alive, until the water evaporates or sinks into the surface of the paper. Interestingly, a small addition of water does not lighten the color too much; it stays a fairly intense color even when floating around in the puddles that we will create. Any India ink will work. I prefer the Dr. Ph. Martin's Bombay India inks since they are the least expensive brand and they have the widest variety of yummy colors.

Materials

BASICS
- Your art journal
- A few sheets from your larger mixed media or watercolor practice paper pad
- Inexpensive small paint brush
- Paper towels
- Nitrile gloves
- Plastic table cover to protect your work surface
- Wax paper to protect your journal pages
- Apron

FOCUS MATERIALS FOR THIS CHAPTER
- One or two bottles of India ink (teal and violet are my favorite colors and play nicely together)
- White cray pas oil pastel
- A small pump spray bottle that can be used for both water and ink
- A small container of water
- A few commercial stencils
- Some found objects to use as masks such as feathers, string or a blade of decorative grass (either real or fake). Be sure the objects can be washed off or discarded.

India Ink Bloom

It is best to explore this ink process on a few practice pages using your larger mixed media or watercolor paper. We are not practicing to get anything "right" but to have fun with truly no expectations. I encourage you to play on the practice page so you can focus on the process and feel free to explore the materials; sometimes doing this outside of the actual journal helps break down the worry about following rules and creating something specific and perfect—and it helps get us in the zone more quickly.

This is a messy, magical technique. Wear your gloves, an apron and roll up those sleeves. Cover your work surface and have lots of paper towels handy. When you see how much fun this technique is, you will want to do some ink blooms directly in your journal. Before you start in your journal, put a small piece of wax paper or a paper towel behind the page you are working on to catch any ink that may roll onto other pages or your table.

To start, fill your spray bottle with water and set aside. Open your India ink and be sure the dropper in the lid works (if not, you can apply the ink with your paintbrush). Now put a drop or two of ink on the page, then spray it with a bit of water while the ink is wet. Oh my! You are creating an ink bloom; isn't it mesmerizing? Have fun and fill the page with blooms.

A few things to keep in mind:
- India ink is permanent when dry so protect your clothes.
- The ink will stain your hands so wear your gloves.
- A lot of water can seem a bit out of control. Be ready to blot up any huge puddles with paper towels as they occur.
- A very wet technique like this may buckle your pages: Don't stress. After the pages dry they will settle down. Closing your journal will help flatten the dry pages, and in the end, wrinkled and buckled pages are lovely because they give the book added dimension.

It is fun to experiment with how much time to let the ink dry before blotting. The longer you wait to blot, the more the ink will seep in to the page and become permanent in that shape. If you blot right away most of the color will lift onto the paper towel. Try leaving areas alone and not blotting at all; these will dry and the ink bloom shapes can be just beautiful. The biggest challenge is your own patience.

Be sure to keep the paper towels you use to blot the ink. We will use these lovely "rags" for

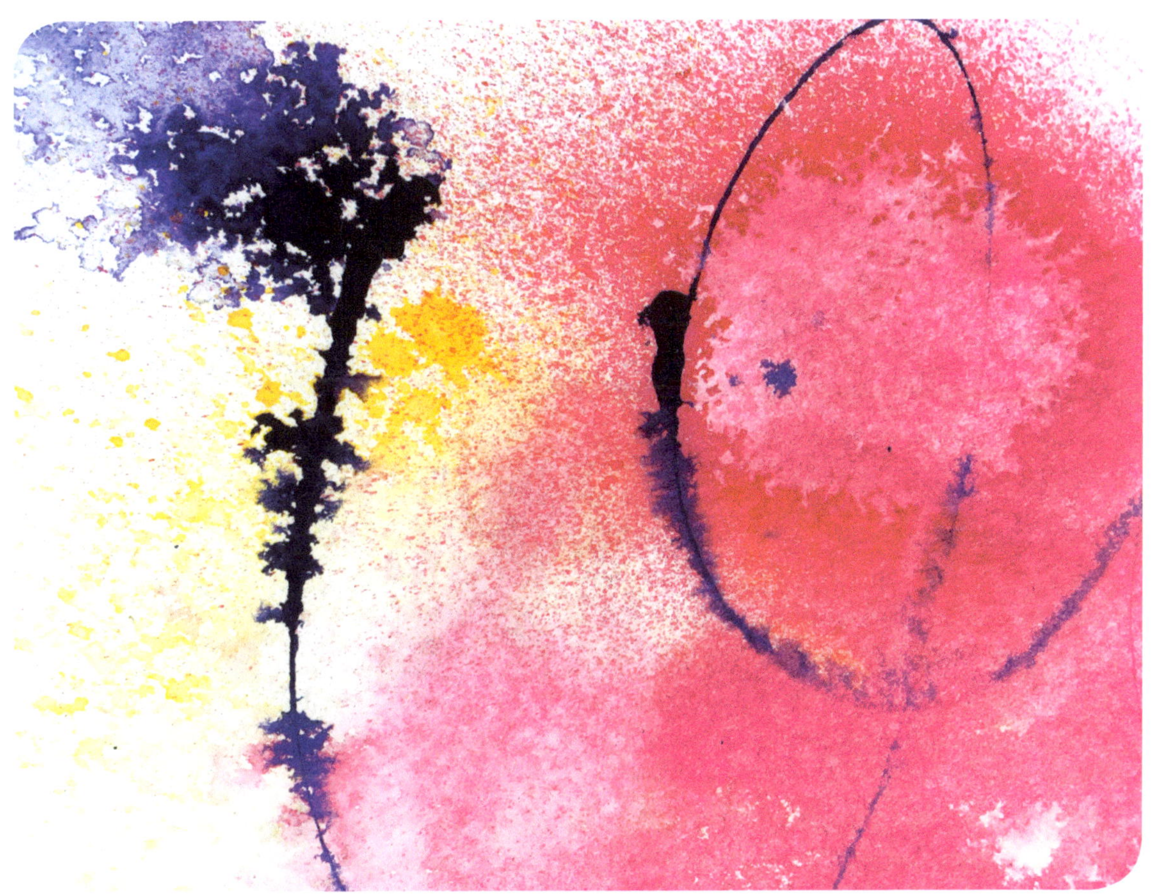

Purple India ink blooms into intriguing shapes when water is added to the wet ink.

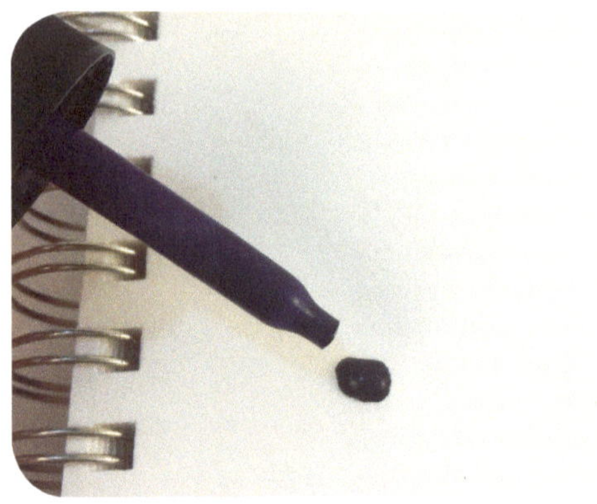

Drop a small amount of India ink onto the page using the dropper or a paintbrush.

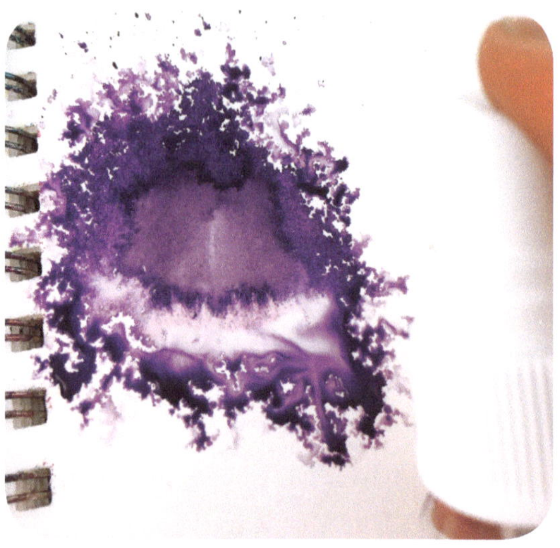

Spritz water from a small pump sprayer onto the drop of ink to make the ink "bloom."

future collage additions.

Now try a reverse approach: Spray the clean water on the page first, then try dripping a bit of ink into the wet spot. The ink should bloom this way as well.

Are you getting into the "what if" state of mind?

What if you drag a clean, wet (with water) paintbrush over your page? Now try dripping a bit of the ink onto the damp lines. Tilt your paper and let the ink and water mix and flow, creating dancing lines. You can also blow on the lines with or without a straw. The blooms will take place within the wet area, so you can make all kinds of crazy lovely designs. This is even more fun with different colors of ink.

I guarantee that you will fall in love with the ink blooms quickly, and it will only take one or two practice pages to get hooked on the ink and water process. I suggest you set these pages aside, let them dry and we will pick them back up to add layers on top of the dried ink blooms with future techniques.

Ink Spray

Another messy, fantastic technique is actually spraying the ink directly onto the page. As with the ink bloom, I suggest covering your work sur-

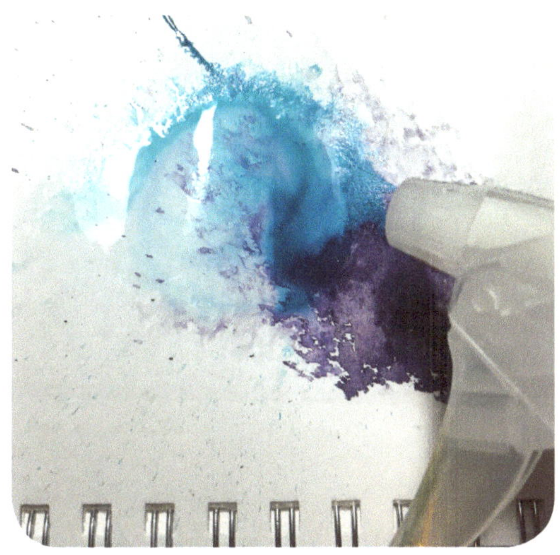

Add another color of ink to create multi-hued blooms.

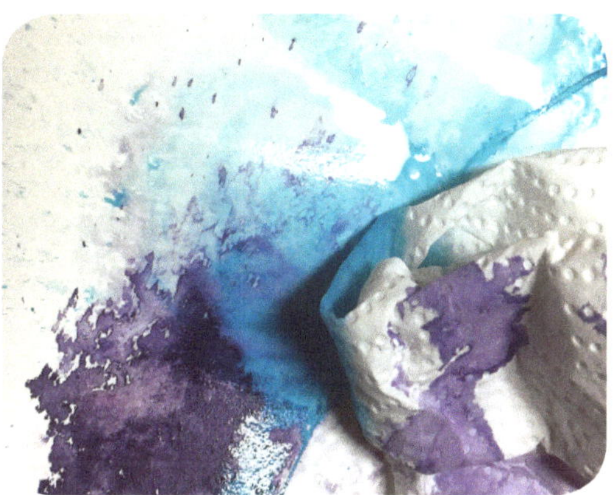

Too much ink on the page? Use a paper towel to blot up the extra.

face, wearing your gloves and apron and having paper towels handy. Continuing to work on a practice page (one of your larger sheets of mixed media or watercolor paper) will add to the fun and focus on the process, not the stress around creating a perfect page at this point.

Carefully pour some ink into an empty spray bottle, filling it about half way. Now try spraying just a bit onto a page (it might take a few pumps to get the spray going). Fun, fun, fun! (You can also add a little bit of water; diluting the ink a bit won't affect the results or the intense color.)

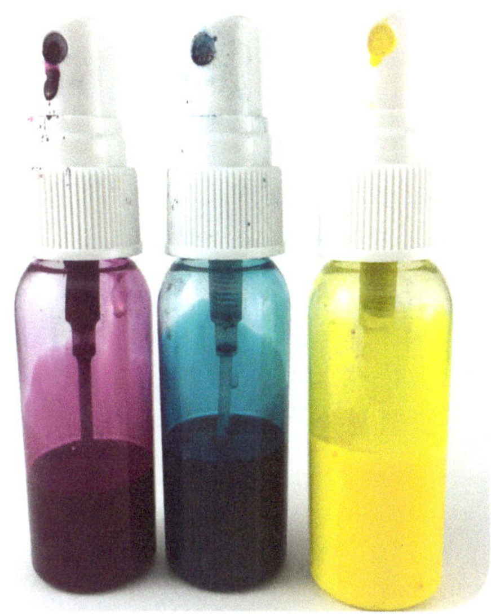

Fill a mini pump spray bottle with ink to create colorful backgrounds.

Try spraying from different distances away from your page. Experiment with leaving some of the page white, or with a very light amount of spray compared to heavier, darker areas. Remember that the longer you wait to blot up the puddles of ink, the more the ink will soak into the paper and become permanent. Playing with drying times can produce different effects.

Using Masks

You can use this spray technique over various masks, just be sure the mask can be washed or disposed of when you are finished. Use household items (like string) or an interesting leaf (either real or plastic) or long piece of grass or wheat growing near your home. Place the object on your page and spray over it. Blot any puddles or large blobs. Remove

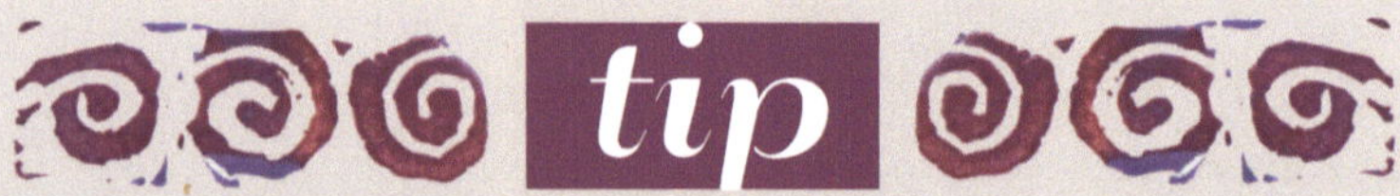

The spray pump mechanism will often clog with ink because the varnish particles are slightly larger and stickier than pigments found in watercolor inks. Simply remove the pump with its tube from the bottle and run it under hot water for a few minutes. Place the tube into a cup of warm, clean water and pump a few times to clear the mechanism. This should un-clog the pump quickly. When finished working, be sure to clean the pump using the process just described. Pour the ink back into its original bottle (replace the dropper screw top securely). Then use hot water to clean any remaining ink out of the pump bottle.

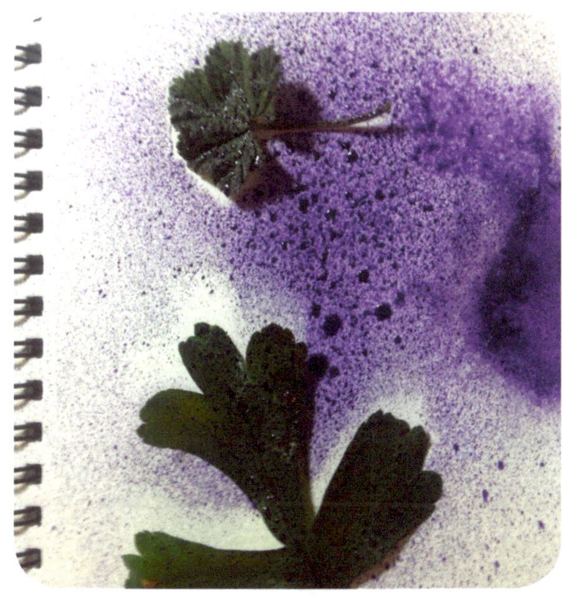

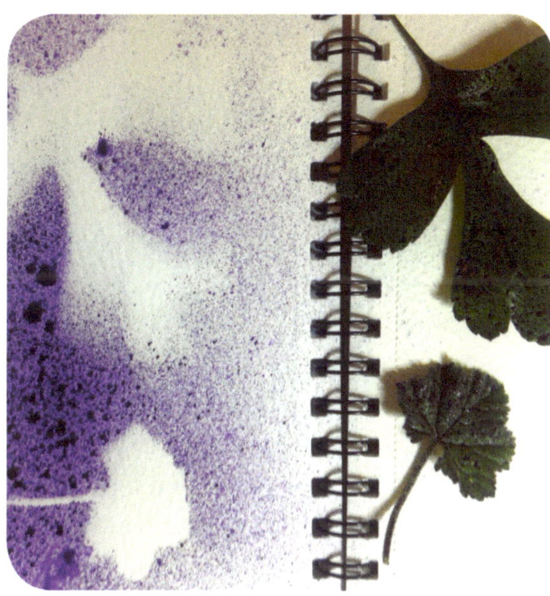

Leaves make interesting masks for art journaling. Lay the leaves on your journal page or practice paper and spray ink over them.

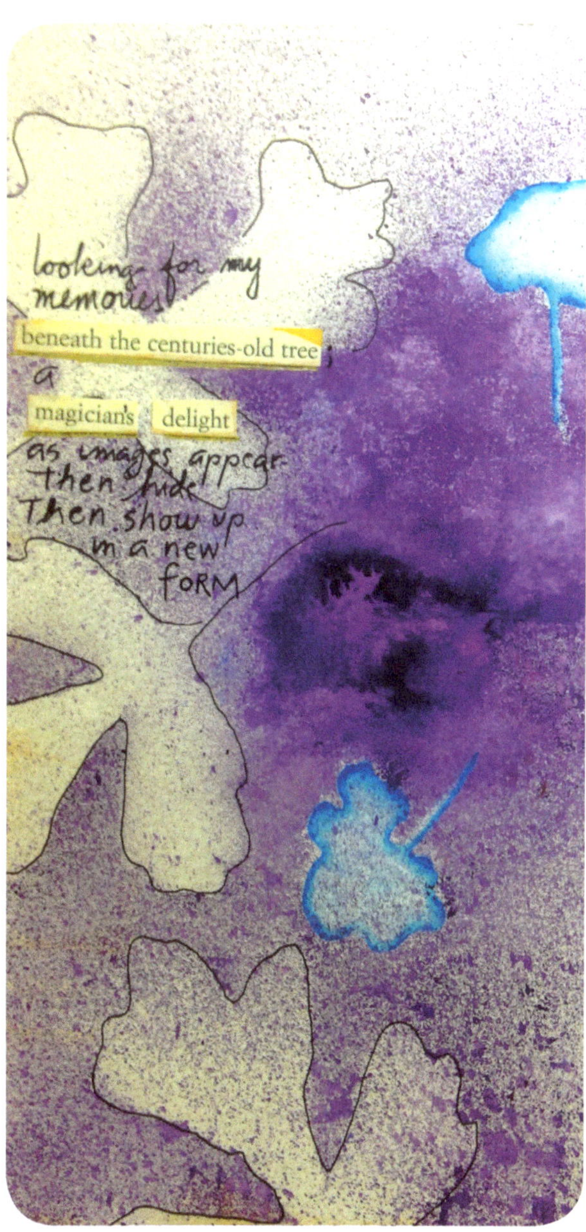

The blank spaces left behind after spraying over a mask are perfect backdrops for text.

the mask and you will be amazed! The page remains white under your mask; the spray adds color around the object. I guarantee you will want to fill many pages this way.

This product has just a slight odor, but it is still a good idea to work in a well-ventilated space.

Time for some what-ifs: What if you use a plastic doily, mesh produce bag, old lace or cardboard cutout as a mask? Anything that is relatively flat and disposable can work. Drywall tape is fun; it is a bit sticky on one side and leaves an interesting grid when used as a mask.

I love using feathers. After I have sprayed over a feather a few times it actually becomes stiff with the dried ink and can easily be glued onto a journal page, so I save the feather for future use.

When you decide to tear yourself away from this technique you can pour the ink from the spray bottle back into the original bottle, then clean the spray bottle thoroughly.

Cray Pas Resist

India ink will also react like watercolor when it flows onto a waxy surface. For this playful experiment you will continue to use the ink, but first make some marks on the large practice paper with your cray pas. Since

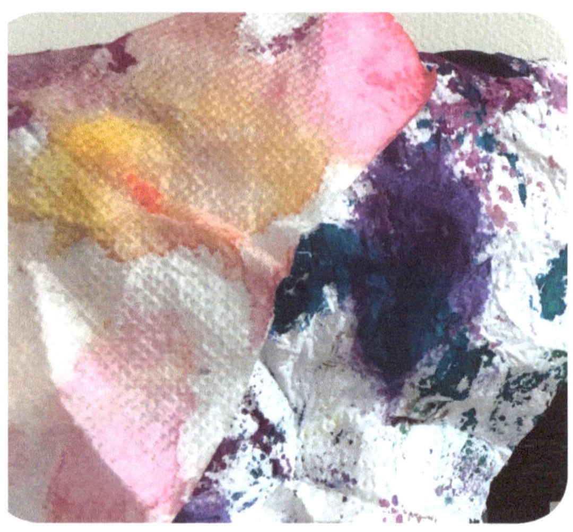

Save the paper towels you use to blot extra ink. They can be used as collage material when dry.

you will be exploring this technique with a white cray pas, it will be a little hard to see. So just throw caution to the wind and make some marks without worrying about how they look. Here are the steps:

1. Make some marks with cray pas on practice paper. Press pretty hard so the wax transfers onto the surface of the paper.

2. Spray some clean water over the cray pas marks just to dampen the paper a tiny bit.

3. Spray or drip some of the ink over the cray pas marks; the magic should appear quickly.

The cray pas oil/wax surface will resist the ink, forcing the ink to move away and not

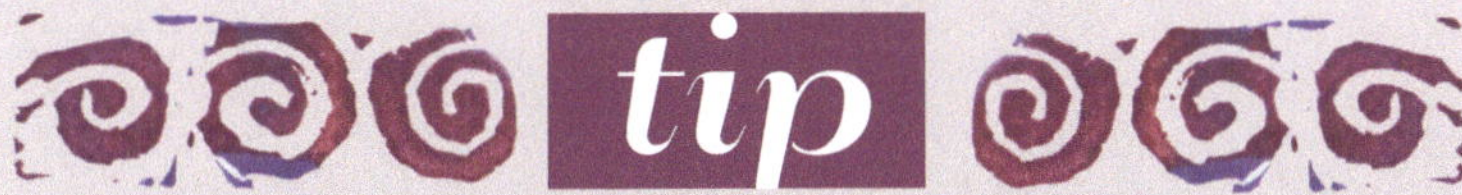

I have found that both the India ink bloom and the spray techniques are fail-proof so long as the paper is heavy enough to cooperate. That is why we are working on either mixed media paper or watercolor paper.

stick to the cray pas marks. This will leave a beautiful texture around the marks, and will create a layered or textured effect quickly.

Any color cray pas will work. You can base your color choice on the color of your ink and find something that will create a nice contrast. I usually stay with white cray pas because I love the contrast. I encourage you to experiment.

If you don't see the white cray pas line showing through the ink it may be due to too much water, which will allow the ink to actually float above the cray pas mark. Blot the area to dry it up a bit, then try adding a smaller amount of ink on top of the cray pas mark.

We have just covered five different ways of working with India ink to create some layers

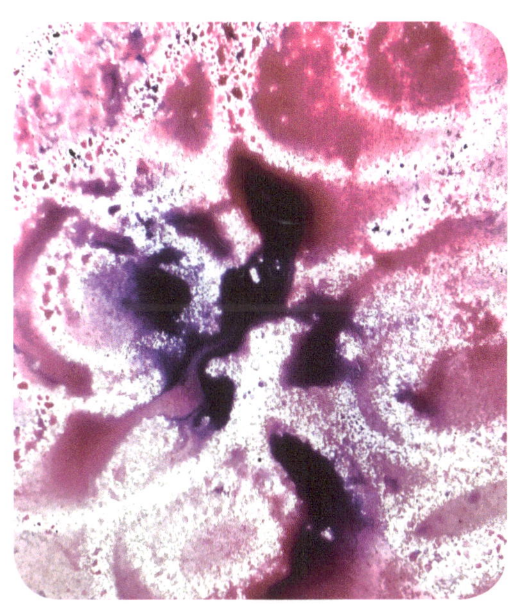

The oil and wax of a white cray pas resists the ink, creating a unique design and texture.

Save all of your paper towels that might have ink on them. I sometimes wet the towels and squish them together to create a sort of tie-dye effect while they are slightly damp (this won't work if the ink is completely dry). Open the towels up and spread them out to dry (be sure you leave them on a covered surface so the ink does not transfer to your table). Once the towels dry they make great collage papers as long as you separate the plies before gluing anything down. When you glue the paper towel down, always put your glue on the book page rather than trying to glue the paper towel, which may cause it to shred.

and textures on our practice pages. At this point, you can set aside the practice pages to dry (we will come back to them in the next chapters and add layers) and you can put the ink techniques directly into your journal.

Working directly in your journal offers the opportunity to create a "first" layer on your pages. You can repeat all of the ink techniques directly on your pages with the following additional considerations:

1. Try to lay your journal open flat (why I love working with a coil binding). Working on both sides of the coil is called creating a "spread." I find it most satisfying to work on both sides. However, some students prefer to stay with the more traditional right side of the book only. Try both approaches to see what you like.

2. Place paper towels or wax paper under the pages you will work on in case the ink starts to slide off the page.

3. If the techniques don't work as well in your journal it is likely due to a paper quality issue. No worries; you can cut up your practice paper and paste parts onto your journal page.

To clean up, rinse off your nitrile gloves and set them aside to dry for future use.

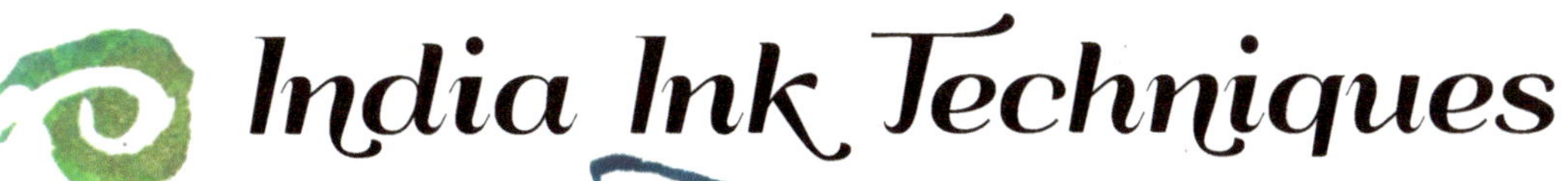

India Ink Techniques

Summary of techniques to explore on
your practice paper:

- Drip ink onto paper, then spray with water

- Wet paper, then drip ink onto wet surface

- Use a brush to paint a wet area, then drip ink along brush
  water line, then tilt paper to let ink flow in lines

- Spray ink directly onto the paper and over stencils and masks

- Create cray pas marks first, dampen the paper over the marks,
  then apply ink over the cray pas to see the resist effect.

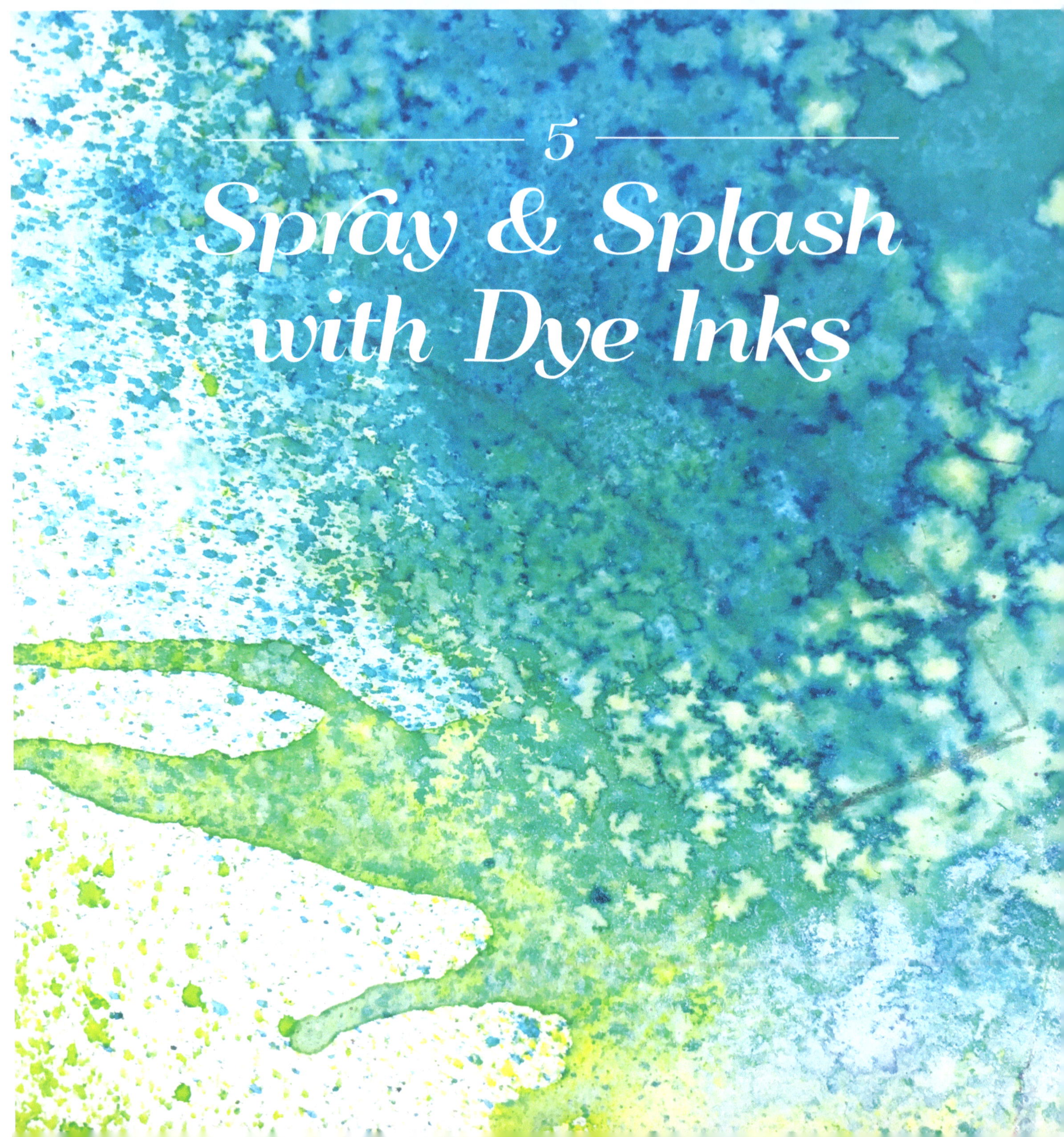
5
Spray & Splash
with Dye Inks

Dye

-based inks are different from India inks in that they remain water-reactive even after they are completely dry. The ability to bleed, move and continue to work on the sprayed surface days and weeks after the first application allows for loads of opportunities to manipulate the colors and textures as we build up the luscious layers on our pages.

These dye inks should be kept off of your skin (wear your nitrile gloves). Your clothes and your work surface should be covered. When spraying directly into your journal, first place a paper towel or waxed paper under the pages that will receive the color to keep it from bleeding onto other pages.

Get ready to enter the creative zone when you unleash the magic of these dye ink sprays.

Basic spray considerations:

- For the absolute most fun, start on a practice page as you did with the India inks. You will practice these techniques

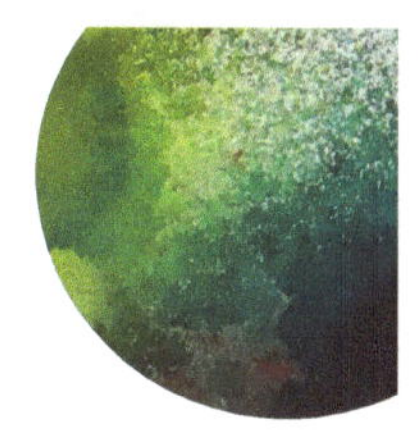

Materials

BASICS
- **Your art journal**
- **A few sheets from your larger mixed media or watercolor paper**
- **Inexpensive small paint brush**
- **Paper towels**
- **Nitrile gloves**
- **Plastic table cover to protect your work surface**
- **Wax paper to protect your journal pages**
- **Apron**

FOCUS MATERIALS FOR THIS CHAPTER
- **Dylusions spray inks**
- **White cray pas oil pastel**
- **A small spray bottle filled with water**
- **A few commercial stencils**
- **Some found objects to use as masks such as feathers, string or a blade of decorative grass (either real or fake). Be sure the objects can be washed off or discarded.**
- **A few tablespoons of table or kosher salt**

on the larger sheet, then see what you'd like to put directly on your journal pages. Working on larger paper outside of your art journal will encourage your curiosity and playfulness.

- If the pump mechanism of the spray bottle clogs (which will happen), just unscrew the cap and lift the pump out of the bottle. Run the pump under hot water for a few seconds, then place it in a cup of warm/ hot water and depress the pump until the spray starts to work again. After you can get some hot water to go through the pump, remove it from the cup and spray it again to get as much water out as possible. Replace it back on the ink bottle, then spray into the sink once or twice to let the ink push out the remaining water. Now you are ready to go.

- Usually only two to four pumps of the ink are needed to fill the whole page. There is no need to create a cloud of spray ink by multiple, fast pumps. You want to avoid having any of the spray ink stay in the air where you are breathing.

- There is no odor associated with this product, but it is still a good idea to work in a well-ventilated space.

- Experiment (as we did with the India ink) with the distance you hold your spray bottle from the page for various effects.
- Have lots of paper towels handy to blot any large puddles.
- Wear your nitrile gloves. If you don't, the inks will stain your hands for a few days.
- These spray bottles are great to up-cycle when they are empty and use as additional water spray bottles for future art adventures.

Using Commerical Stencils

There are lots of commercial stencils on the market with designs ranging from patterns to recognizable images. I prefer to use stencils with interesting patterns as they allow for a greater range of use and interpretation. The patterns make wonderful bottom, middle or top layers. Some of the stencils with sayings or cute images are a bit limiting.

Commercial stencils are made from a thin plastic sheet, and they lay flat against your journal page. You can make your own stencils by cutting out images and designs from old file folders or cover stock paper, but you won't be able to wash these paper stencils off and re-use them like plastic stencils. Sheets of plastic are sold just for this purpose, but I have found it

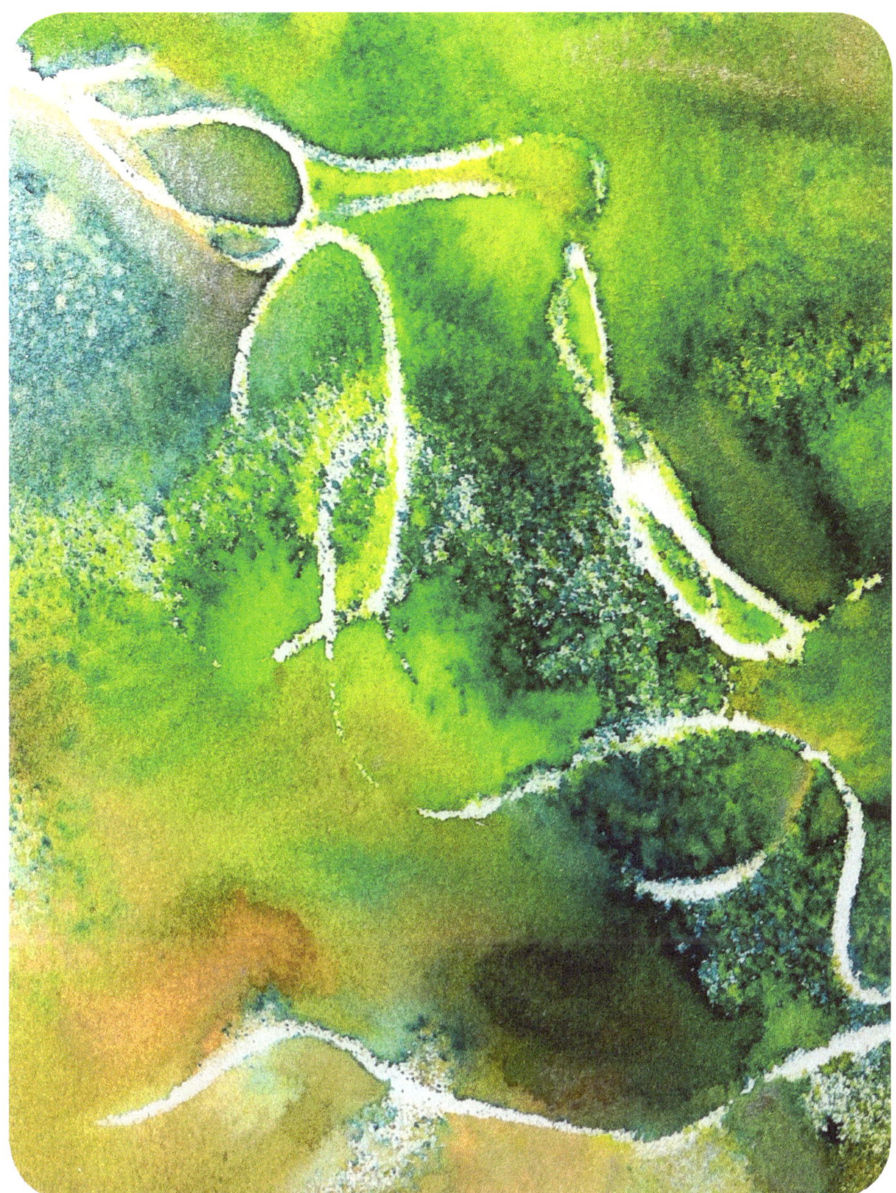

Spray various colors of ink to see how they mix and blend. Spraying over a string or yarn will leave fascinating marks behind.

tedious to cut my own stencils when there are so many ready-made to choose from at a reasonable price.

You can find great stencils online, or in the scrapbook section of your local craft store. Consider the size of your journal page when choosing a stencil. Most of my stencils are 6 by 6 inches square.

The Basic Spray Process

1. Select a stencil and place it on your paper.
2. Select an ink color, then swirl the bottle to mix the solution. Swirling is better than full-on shaking, which can cause the particles to clog the pump a bit faster or can throw some of the wet ink directly onto your walls.
3. Point the spray bottle toward your page, about 6 to 8 inches above the paper and push the pump once or twice. Be ready to blot any large drips (with paper towel) that might have landed (if you think you'd like to lift them) or embrace the blobs and keep spraying.
4. Vary the distance away from the page to see the different effects. Remember, you likely only need a few pumps to fill your page.
5. Lift your stencil off the page and place it on a paper towel. Blot the stencil (or run it under water) to clean off the excess ink.

Option: If the stencil looks fairly wet with color you can flip it over onto a spot on your page (or in your journal) and—using your gloved hand—press down on the back of the stencil to push the excess color onto the page. This is basically printing with the stencil. Just to tickle your brain: Printing with the stencil this way creates a "negative" image, as if you were using a mask.

6. Experiment with blotting the wet ink left on the page. The blotted area will give you a lighter, textured area different from the direct spray.

Fabulous, no? Couldn't you just spray all day? The colors will mix and blend; when you blot away excess you may end up with new colors and textures left by the paper towels.

Commercial stencils give quick and dependable results. Try a layered approach. When the first layer of spray is a bit dry, put a different stencil over the page and spray. The colors will mix, as the first layer of dye ink is water-reactive. Experiment with blotting to see how this affects the color mixing.

Spraying Over Found Objects

Time to open those wonderful "ephemera drawers" (aka: junk drawers). Do you have one or two? Look for objects with interesting shapes that are relatively flat and something you can either rinse off or throw away. Caution: Do not spray over anything that will come in contact with food.

Some of my favorites:
- String (or thick threads)
- Feathers of any kind
- Produce net bags (like the kind that garlic is sold in)
- Keys
- Long grasses found near my house in the middle of summer, or tree leaves that fall as the seasons turn
- Plastic forks
- Paper clips

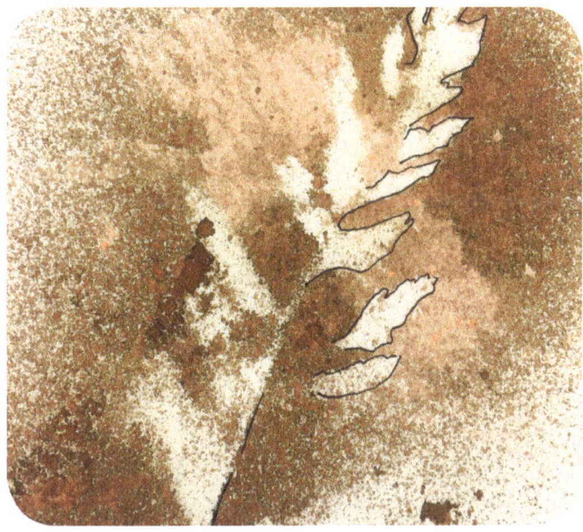

Forage for leaves, grasses or other natural items to use as masks when spraying ink in your art journal.

Using Salt for Texture

There is a common watercolor practice of sprinkling a bit of table or kosher salt into a puddle of wet watercolor and allowing that area to dry. The salt crystals repel the pigments in the color and push them away while absorbing the water, leaving tiny areas of crystalline shapes. Dylusions spray inks will react the same way to salt.

Try this:
1. Use the spray inks in any of the ways already described.
2. While the inks are still shiny-wet (but not in big puddles), sprinkle varying amounts of salt directly onto the colored areas.
3. Allow to completely dry, then wipe the salt off (you may have to wipe vigorously or use a dry sponge). The salt will leave a very cool texture, which will be most obvious if you use the salt over darker colors. (If you rub the salt off the paper with your bare fingers the Dylusions ink will stain your fingers.)
4. An alternative to try: First sprinkle salt on the clean, dry page. Then spray over the salt. Let the ink dry for a few hours (or overnight). Wipe away the salt with a paper towel.

Using Cray Pas Resist

I discovered that the Dylusions ink will not adhere to a waxy surface, and the cray pas resist technique described in chapter 4 with the India inks works with these inks as well:

1. Make some marks on your practice paper with the white cray pas (remember to press hard on the cray pas).
2. Spray over the cray pas with any of your colors.
3. Use paper towels to blot up puddles.

After the Party

Once the spray inks are dry, you can move and blend the colors using a wet paint brush.

Try this:

Apply Dylusions spray on a page using any of the techniques already described and let dry. Dip a small paintbrush into some clean water. Drag your wet paintbrush over the spray ink in a small area to experiment with how the ink will "re-activate" and move based on how you move your paint brush.

Try creating some patterns by placing a commercial stencil back on top of the ink, then touching your wet paintbrush into the

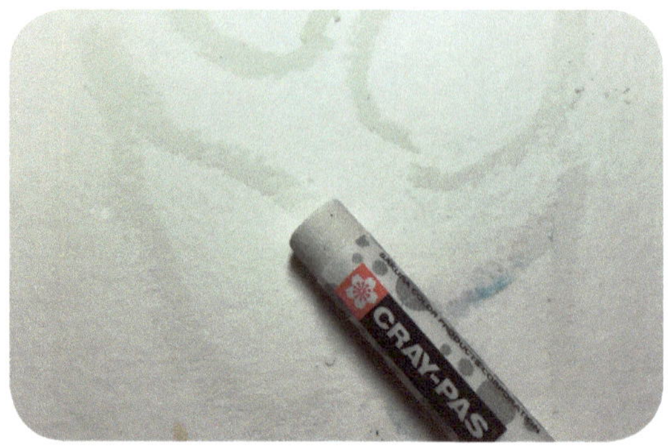

Use the cray pas to make marks freely on your practice paper or journal page.

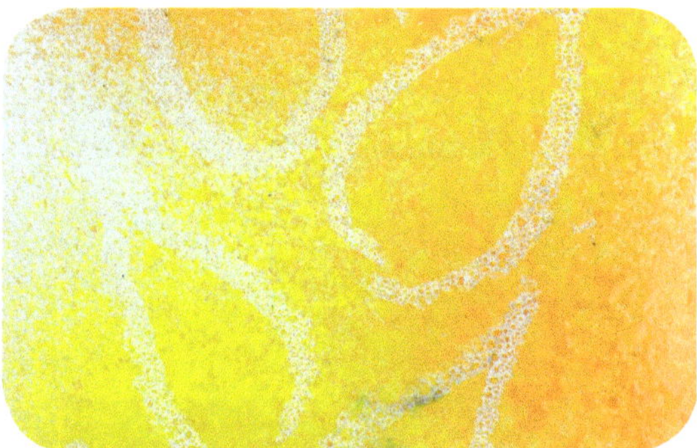

Spray ink over the cray pas marks.

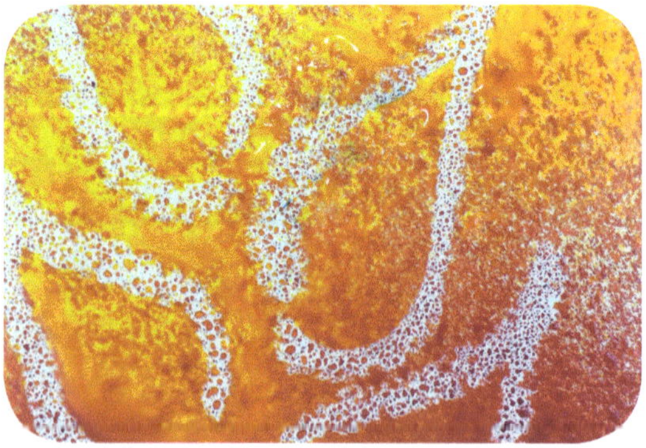

The cray pas marks will resist the ink. You can spray additional colored inks over the marks, too.

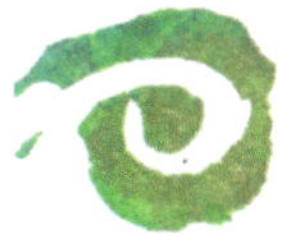 # Beyond Breakfast

One time I was with my journal group at breakfast and we got a bit carried away...we set down leftover breakfast food on our pages and had a blast with spray inks. The little potato bits did nothing but the orange peels were terrific! Plastic forks and spoons were fun, too. In the silly zone for sure. (Clearly, none of the sprays should be ingested, so save this experiment until the end of the meal, when the table is protected, and only use on items that are bound for the recycle bin or garbage bag.)

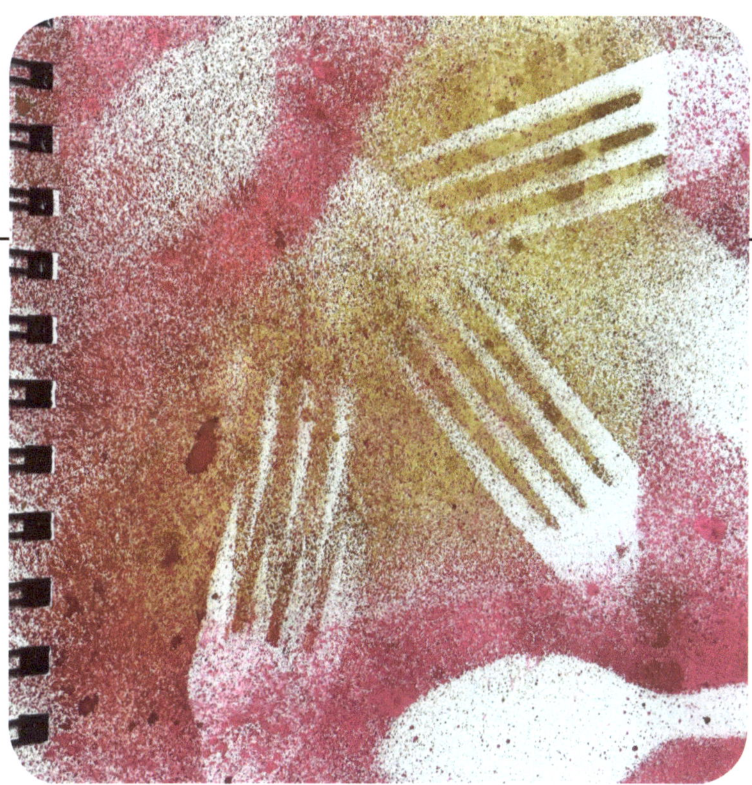

cut out areas of the stencil. If the paint brush is very wet, and you create a little puddle of water, use a paper towel to pick up the wet ink.

Lift the stencil and admire the (sometimes subtle) effects of pulling up the ink.

Once you have explored these techniques on your practice pages, set them aside to dry. Now you can spray the Dylusion inks directly onto your journal pages. I like to spray random pages in a new journal without regard to sequence. Later, when I open the book to that sprayed page it is always fun to see how the color and textures of the spray (that may have been done a long time ago) seem to fit the moment of that journal entry. Adding background color to random pages is called "preparing" your journal pages and is a great way to get over WPA (white page anxiety). You will see how easy it is to get into the flow without concerns about producing something perfect or amazing on each page.

The Zone of Delight

When I show my students these spray techniques, I love to step back and observe how the creative zone invites us in. There is something magical about the whole process—seeing forms emerge, colors combine and texture develop. And everyone

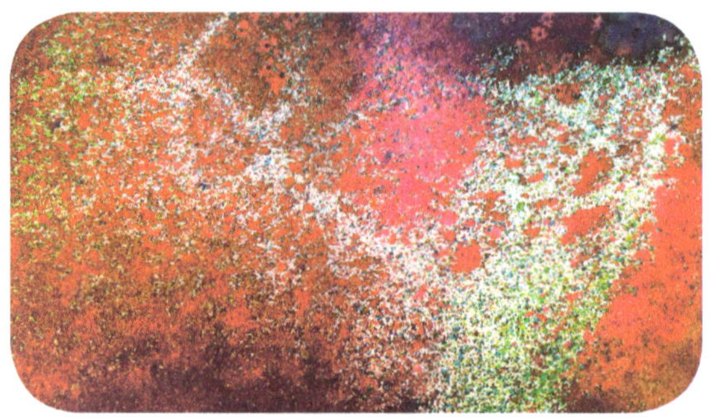

Try spraying ink on random pages in your new journal without regard to sequence to prepare the pages for later use.

is successful. There is no room for failure as we can just keep spraying until we reach that joyful place.

Check in with yourself after a session of spraying and playing with the color and texture on a practice page or directly in your journal. Did time stand still? Did you find yourself asking "what if"?

Sometimes I call a moment within the creative zone a "zone of delight." I am referring to a micro burst of happiness; a time when you recognize you are in the zone, or in the flow of the creative process. Mainly I just like the sound of "zone of delight" as it seems to express the endless, surprising effects these loose, free techniques can produce. For me, it is always delightful to let go, spray up a few pages, sprinkle some salt randomly and blot puddles with paper towels on a whim.

Dye Spray Techniques

In this chapter we played with the following techniques, exploring Dylusions Spray Inks:

- Spraying over stencils

- Spraying over found objects (masks)

- Spraying over salt, or spraying first then adding salt into the wet areas

- Spraying over cray pas marks to create a resist effect

- Going back into the sprayed area (after it is dry) with a wet paint brush to see the effects of lifting, or blending the ink with added water

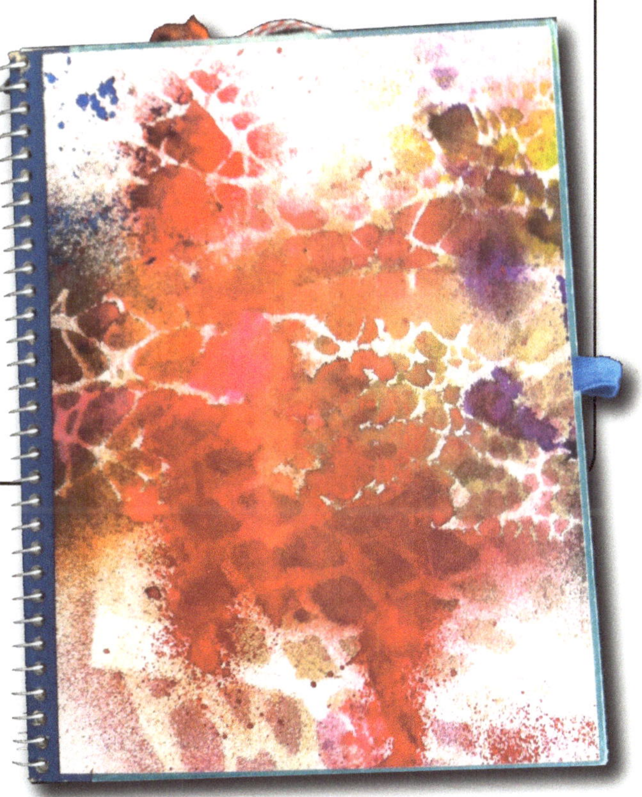

6

Chalk Surprises

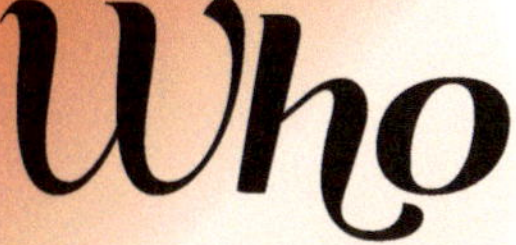

Who doesn't love the rich, vibrant colors of chalk pastels? But, oh my, the mess! These chalks are not traditionally used in art journaling because they present so many challenges around dust control. If you pick one up and swipe it across a page, it is likely to smudge and transfer to other areas as soon as you close your book, and your fingers end up covered in pastel, making it hard to keep any other pages clean.

But wait; don't throw away your pastels just yet. I have found a new way to apply the pastels that eliminates the dust, the smudge factor and the migration of color to areas you don't want colored.

Here's the simple, simple, simple technique. Let's try this directly on a journal page (rather than on a practice sheet).

The Basic Application Process

1. Rub a cotton cosmetic pad (round or square) over the side of a pastel stick that has the label peeled off, or a stick

Materials

BASICS
- Your art journal

FOCUS MATERIALS FOR THIS CHAPTER
- A small set of chalk pastels, preferably sticks with no paper labels on them (be sure these are chalk pastels; this technique will not work with oil pastels)

- Cotton rounds (or squares)

- An eraser

- A commercial stencil with a simple design and larger openings

- Index card (any size) or shipping tag

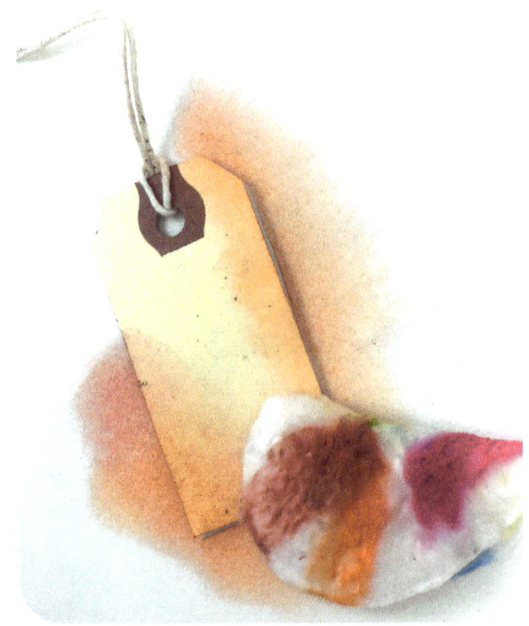

Swipe a cotton round across the pastel to pick up some of the pigment, then swirl it along the edges of a shipping tag.

When you lift off the tag, you will have a blank space on your page with a soft chalk outline.

that is in the set with no individual label. Don't hold the pastel in your hand; instead, leave it sitting in the box along with all the other colors. This eliminates getting the pastel on your skin or all over your fingers.

2. Check the cotton, you should see that the pigment transfers to the cotton easily.

3. Now rub the cotton (where the color is) in swirling, circular motions along the borders of a page. The color will transfer in a soft, blended manner.

4. Play around with different ways to stroke the color onto the page; the marks you create can be blended, layered and controlled fairly easily.

After you have played with the application process, created a border on a journal page and discovered how simple and efficient this process is, you can explore various what-ifs:

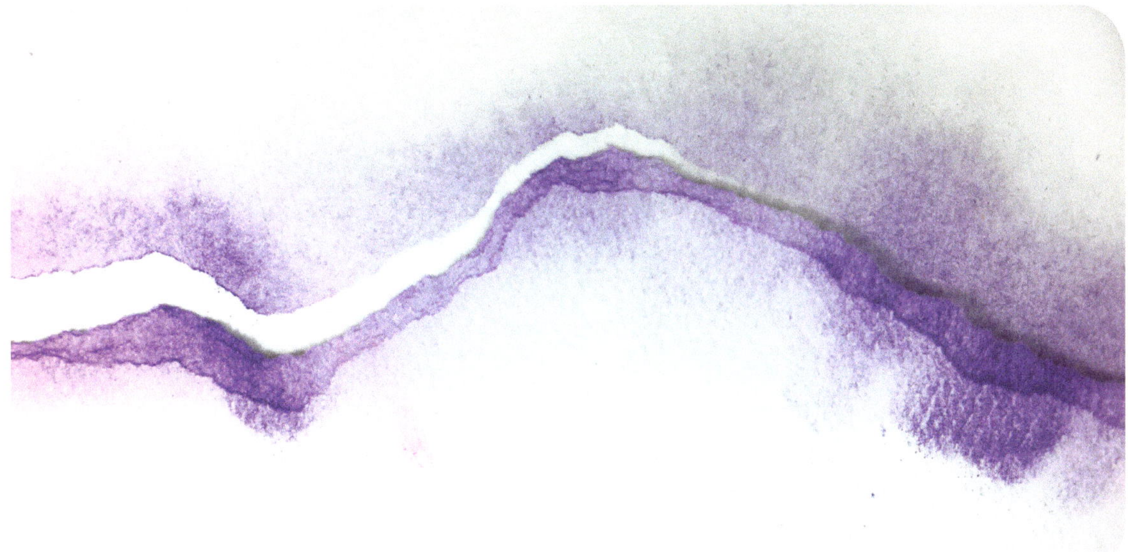

Rub chalk along the torn edge of a piece of paper to create a mountain-like shape.

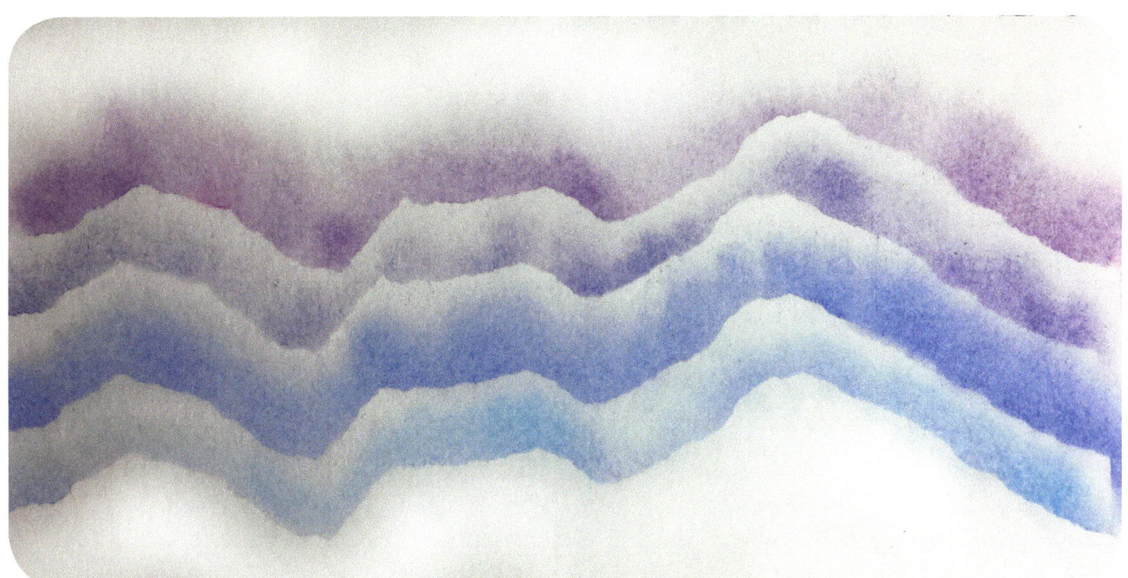

Move the torn piece of paper down the page and repeat the chalk pastel rubbing with a different color to give the effect of a mountain range or a sunset.

1. What if you use an eraser? Put down some pastel color on a page using the cotton pad method described above. Use any eraser (simple pencil erasers are fine) and erase away the pastel in small areas. The eraser lets you pick up some of the color and create a reverse pattern or white lines going through the color.

2. Set down a tag or index card on top of your journal page. Get some pastel color onto your cotton pad, then rub the cotton over the edges of the card (start about 1/8 inch on the inside of the card, swipe out, over the edge and onto the journal page). Lift the card up and you will see the chalk has picked up the edge of the card shape, and softly blended out away from that edge. In this manner, you are using the card as a mask.

3. My favorite: Rip a small piece of paper into a simple mountain shape, creating an uneven (deckled) edge. Set the ripped paper down on your journal page and use it as a mask. (Swipe the cotton over the pastel to pick up the pigment, then rub the cotton over the ripped edge of the paper. Lift the paper to see the lovely soft, blended mountain shape.) Try moving the ripped paper a little bit up or down, over the chalk mark, and repeat the blending with different colors. When you do this multiple times with the same torn paper scrap you can achieve an unusual atmospheric effect: It can look like a sunset or like mist in between mountains.

4. Apply your chalk marks with the cotton directly over a commercial stencil. This works well if the stencil has larger openings. Closed areas of the stencil will preserve the color of the paper, allowing the chalk to show up in the open areas of the stencil's design.

5. Another favorite: Create a chalk mandala on a page by moving a hand-ripped piece of paper, or your commercial stencil, in a circular fashion radiating out from a central point. Try changing colors each time you chalk over the stencil.

6. One last favorite: I like to use the chalks over a small rectangle cut from an index card. This gives the box a soft outline, and leaves a box the white of the journal page. If I line these boxes up in a grid I can use them to represent days of the week (or any other time interval). Great for calendars! Have you experienced getting into that

Chalk Techniques

I know you will love the variety of effects you can get with this chalk application. I have described six of my favorite techniques for you to try on six different pages in your art journal:

- Basic application used to create a chalk border

- Using an eraser to pull up the chalk, leaving a negative space showing through

- Using a card or tag as a mask; create a calendar

- Apply the chalk over a commercial stencil

- Apply the chalk over a ripped piece of paper

- Create a mandala (or circular) design on your page with your ripped piece of paper or a stencil

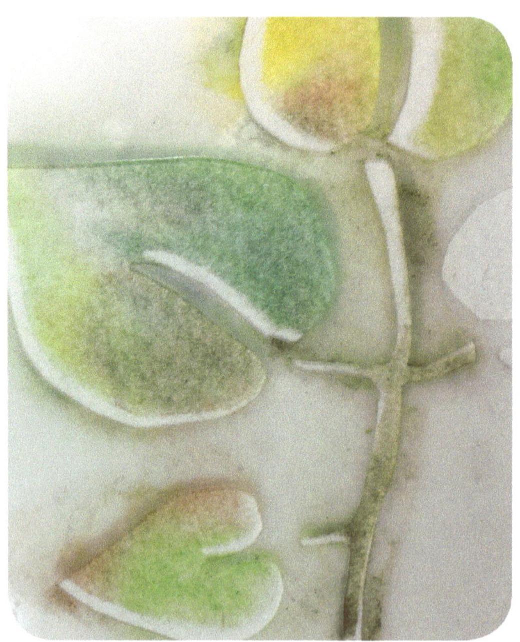

Use chalk pastels in several different colors to fill in a stencil, like this plastic one with a leaf pattern.

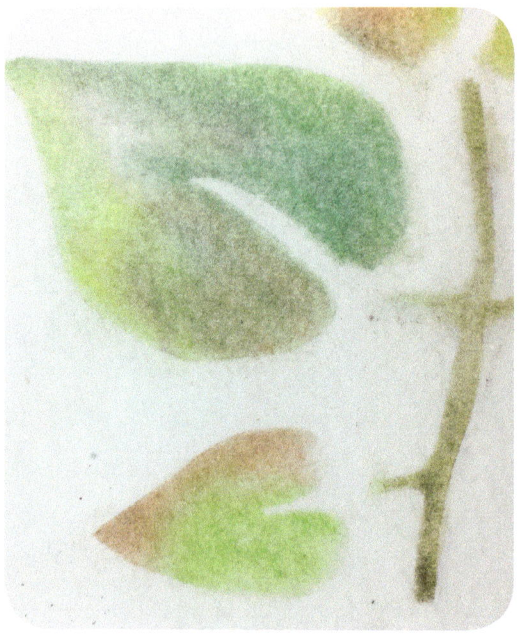

Lift the stencil to reveal the leaf design with softly blended colors.

time-less, deeply engaging zone with these techniques? When I prepare pages and start to breathe life into my art journal I find myself turning the pages frequently, which feels like I'm pulling a warm blanket of creative flow tight around my shoulders. I hope that you have not over-thought your pages, but, instead, you just enjoyed the process of putting some marks and color in a few, random spots. I hope the process has been relaxing, as we have wandered far away from considering the product. We have been working on page preparation rather than taking the time to finish one page at a time before moving on to the next page.

Page preparation you say? Yes. Do you now see that you can take away white-page anxiety (WPA) by doing some of these fun, quick

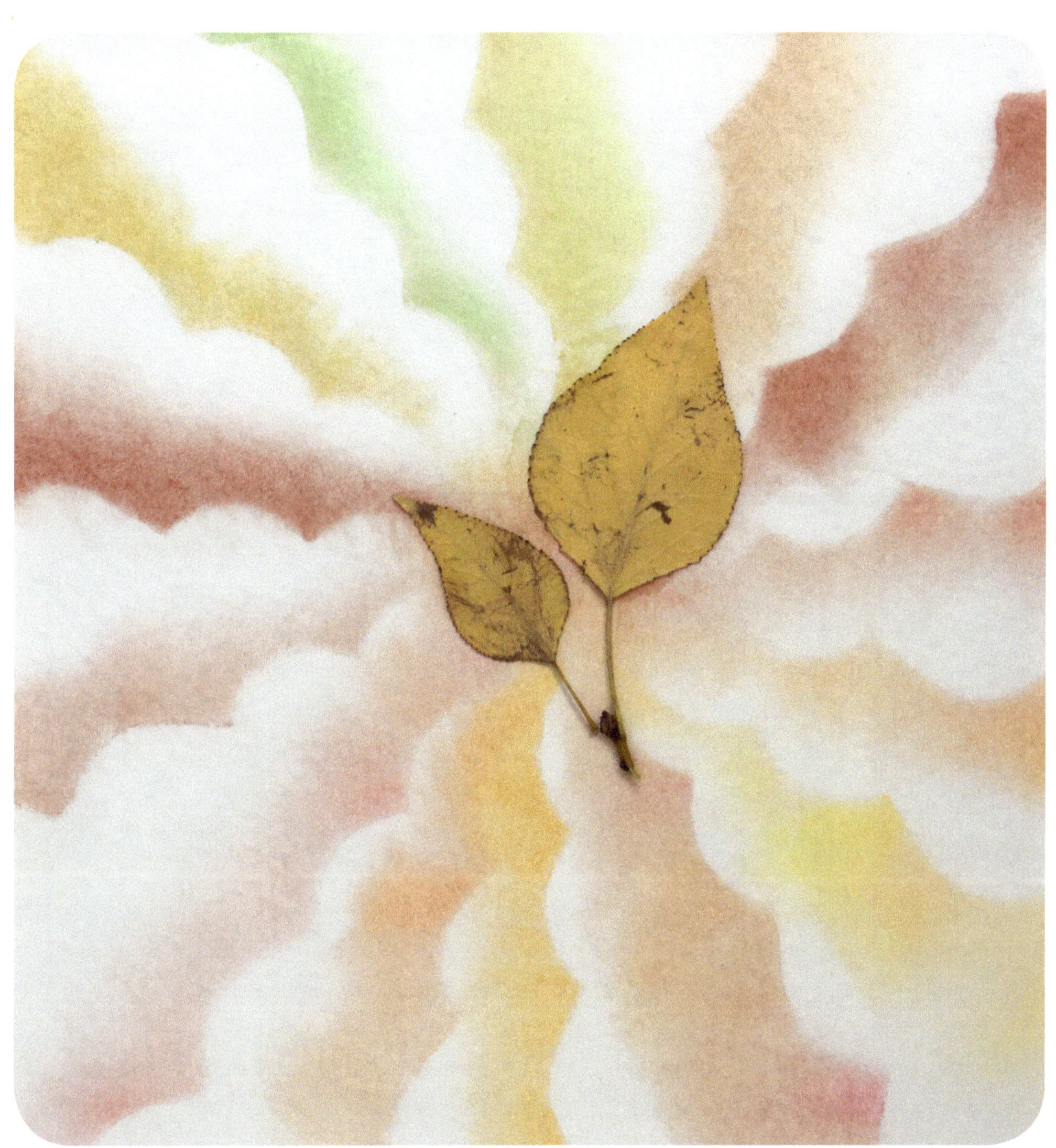

Make a mandala by rubbing chalk pastels in various colors along the edge of a torn piece of paper that's rotated around a central point.

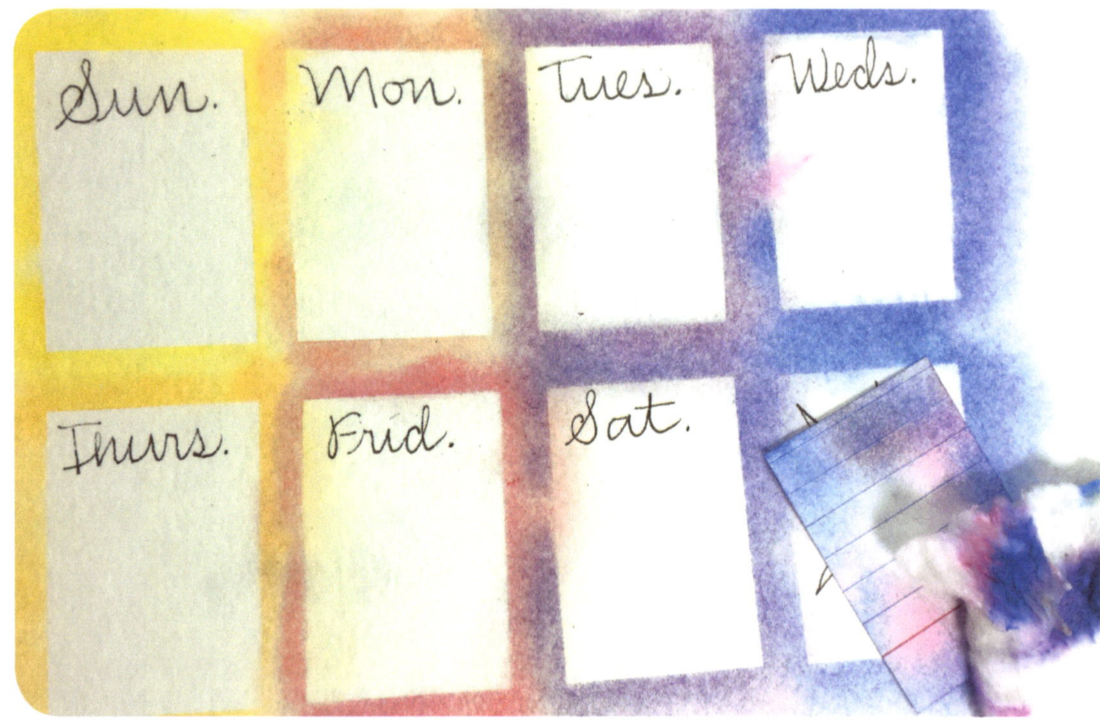

To add a calendar grid to a journal page, use a rectangular piece of index card or paper as a mask for chalk pastel rubbing.

techniques as first layers, or preparations? Creating these first layers seems to be a huge breakthrough for many of my students. You don't have to start a new book with a fabulous, planned art journal page as page 1. You can literally open the book, start to spray or chalk or cray pas just as the mood hits, then close the book. When you re-open it a few days later you will be thrilled to see a few pages begun with fun first layers. Ahhhh, big sigh. No pressure! Remember that our goal is to turn the page, not perfect anything.

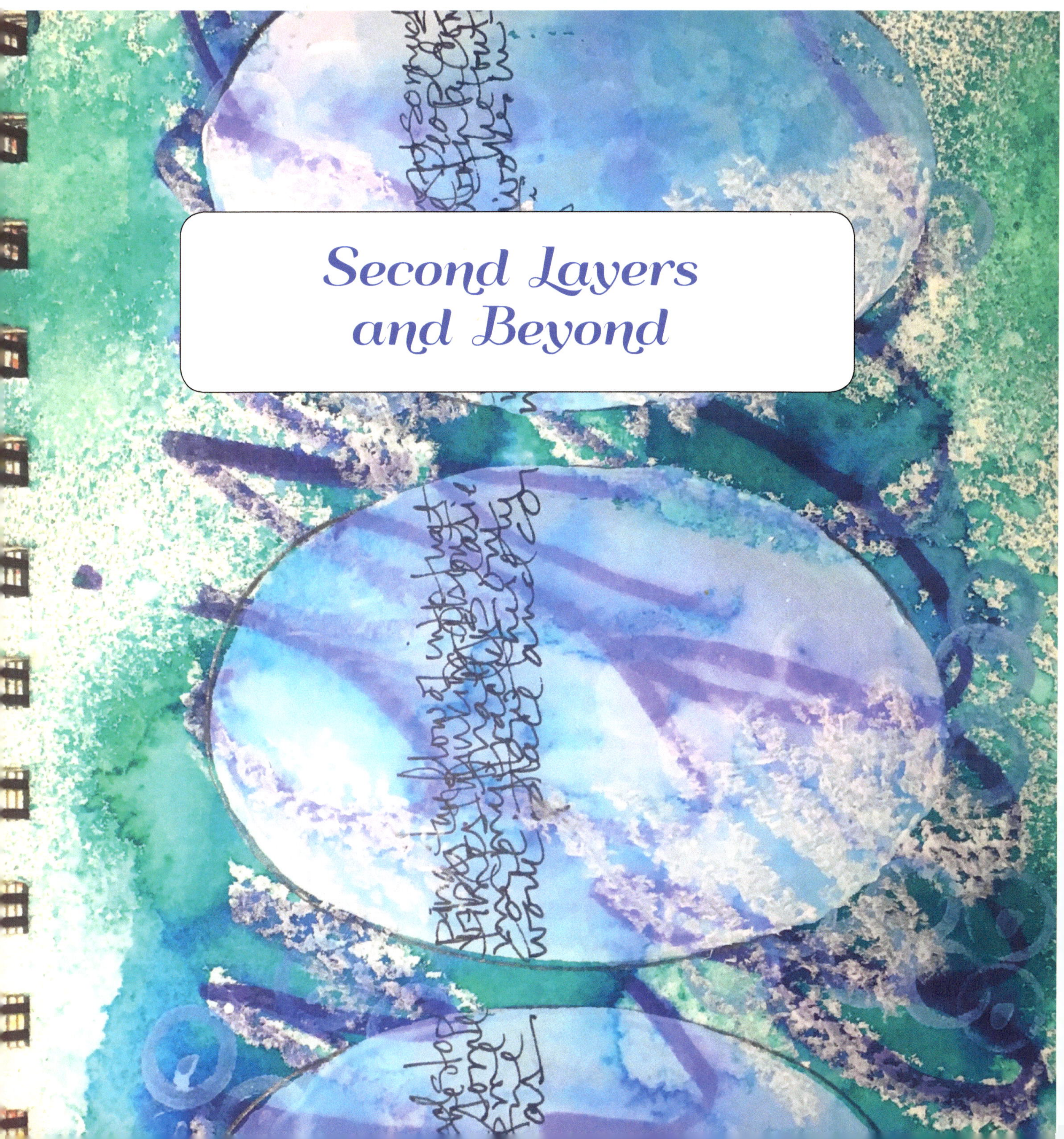

Second Layers and Beyond

7

Collaborations
Chalk + Ink + Stamps

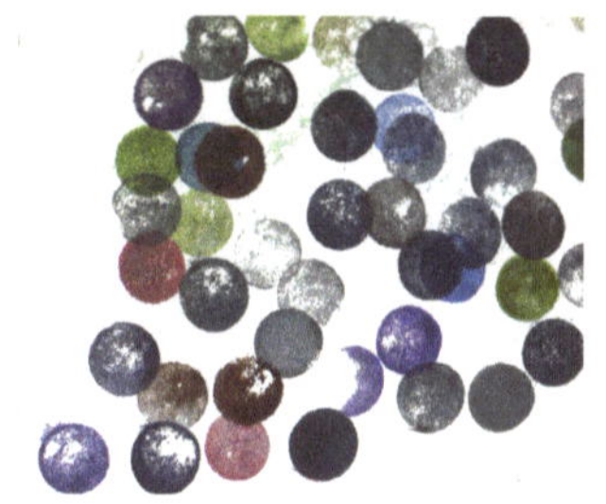

In the previous three chapters, I introduced some of the basic techniques that I love to use in my art journals. India ink, Dylusion spray inks and chalks all produce very different effects, all offer different amounts of control and all lend themselves to the "what if" approach. Time will stand still when you are working with any of these. Set your phone alarm if you have to pick up kids or get dinner started!

What if we combine these three techniques? We will build luscious layers and textures directly in our journals and use our practice pages as collage material.

The India ink, Dylusions inks and chalk techniques all created a first layer on your journal pages and on the practice paper. These first layers prepare your journal pages for additional creative expression. We can play on top of these layers without worry about creating something "perfect."

In this collaboration chapter we will create second layers by combining a few techniques and using rubber stamps to add interest.

Materials

BASICS

- **Practice pages you completed in chapters 4 and 5**
- **Your art journal**

FOCUS MATERIALS FOR THIS CHAPTER

- **Chalk pastels**
- **A glue stick, any brand (don't use re-positional glue as it does not seem to stick well)**
- **Roll of masking tape**
- **Scissors**
- **One push pin, thumb tack or book awl**
- **Decorative brad or fastener**
- **Decorative tape**
- **A variety of rubber stamps with patterns or textures as the stamp design**
- **A variety of "found" stamps; items that can be placed on the inkpad and possibly discarded after use, such as pencil erasers, pieces of a silicone trivet or bubble wrap**
- **A variety of stamp inkpads (such as Distress pads by Ranger, any color or pigment ink by Momento, any dye inkpad)**
- **Paper or cardstock tags**

India Ink + Chalk

Let's start by applying chalk to the (dried) practice pages we created as we explored the India ink techniques.

Looking at your practice page, find an area where you can still see the white of the page (that might be where you sprayed over a feather or another object). Apply some chalk to that white area using a cotton pad and the swipe technique described in chapter 6. You are in for a surprise! The soft, pastel-ly effect of the chalk application works as a lovely contrast to the strong colors and the textures of the inks.

I find chalk pastel to be the perfect second layer. I might have loved the crazy ink blooms, but once the chalk is applied I go directly to heaven. The build-up of contrasting, or different, layers almost "tastes" good! Do you see an area where you sprayed the ink over a stencil (either commercial or found)? The chalks will fill in the paper that was covered by the stencil originally. You can control the chalk application to create an "ombre" effect easily or you can stick with just one color to add contrast to the ink color and texture.

Apply the chalks on top of the cray pas resist on any of the practice pages; the chalk will stick to the waxy-oil of the cray pas and add texture. I love the random results.

Repeat this chalk application on sections of your Dylusion ink practice pages: The same pleasing results are possible with just a piece of cotton picking up some chalk pigment, then rubbing the pigment onto the page. Again, adding the chalk creates a second visual layer.

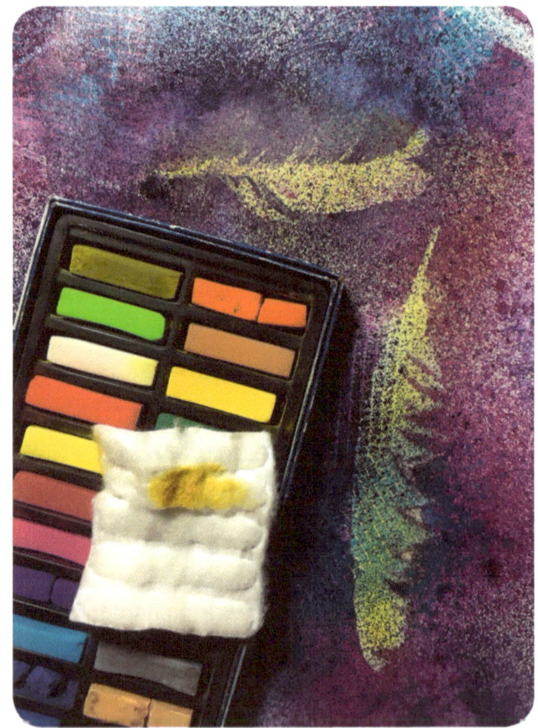

Use a cotton square to lift color from a chalk pastel and rub it onto the journal page.

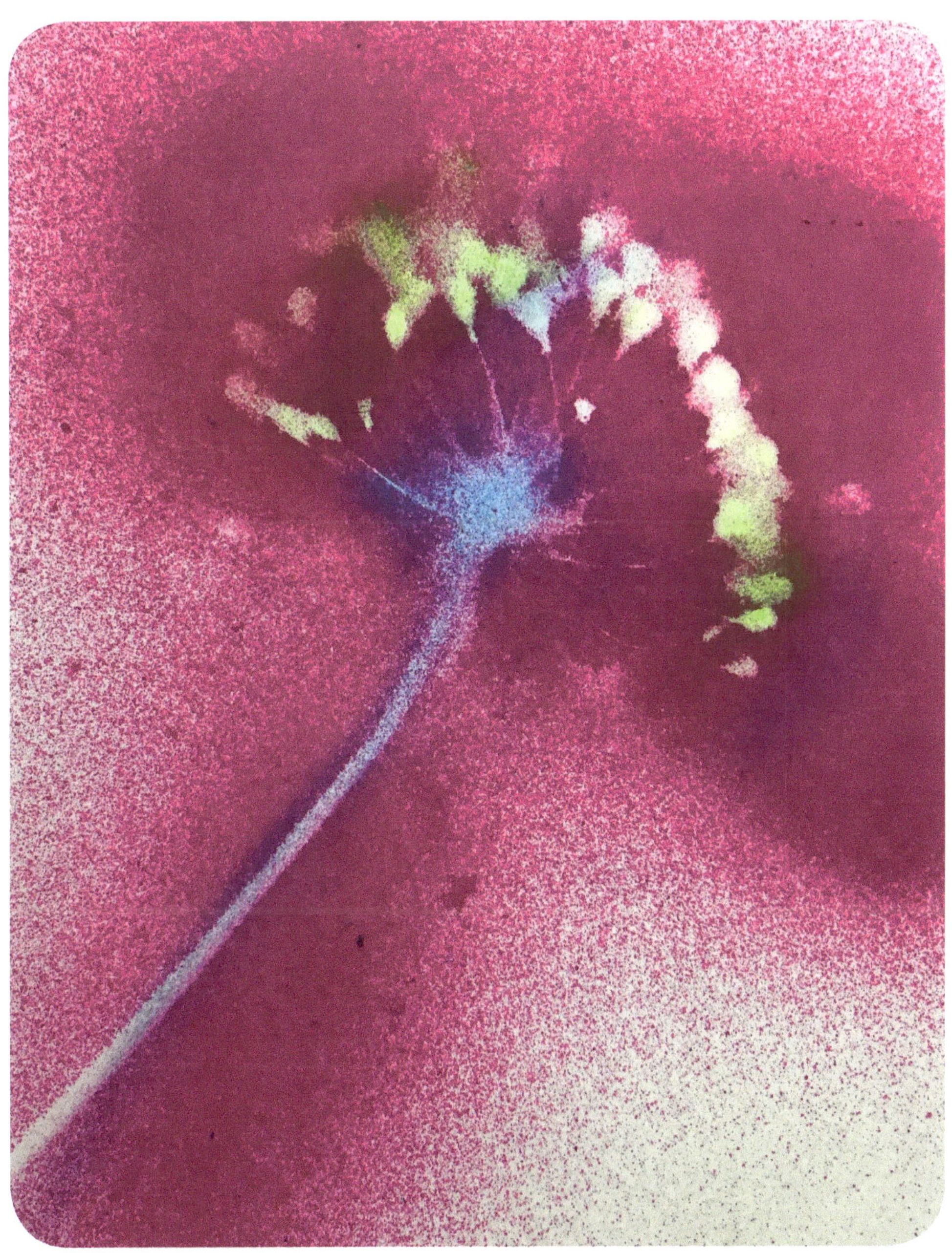

After spraying over a dandelion head, I added colored chalk to the white spaces.

You can add chalk to any of the prepared pages that are in your art journal (the pages with India ink or Dylusions inks). You are becoming a master at layering!

Just as the chalk created a second layer on top of the India or Dylusions ink, the rubber stamps can create a third layer if used on top of everything.

Ink + Chalk + Rubber Stamps

Lots and lots of folks got into the rubber stamp craze and purchased hundreds of darling stamps and inkpads. I was a proud member of that club. While I love the magic of watching an image emerge from stamping, I got a little tired of the limitations most of the stamps put on my self-expression. So I set off to find alternatives to the cute images and ways of using stamping to foster unique expression.

Guess what was on my desk? A wine cork! More on that in a minute.... For now, let's talk inkpads.

There are two main kinds of rubber stamp inkpads, plus a new hybrid.

Pigment inkpads have ink that is a bit sticky. The pigment ink often gives a silky, opaque finish and may be used on a variety of surfaces. Pigment ink is totally permanent after it dries. Pigment ink should be cleaned off

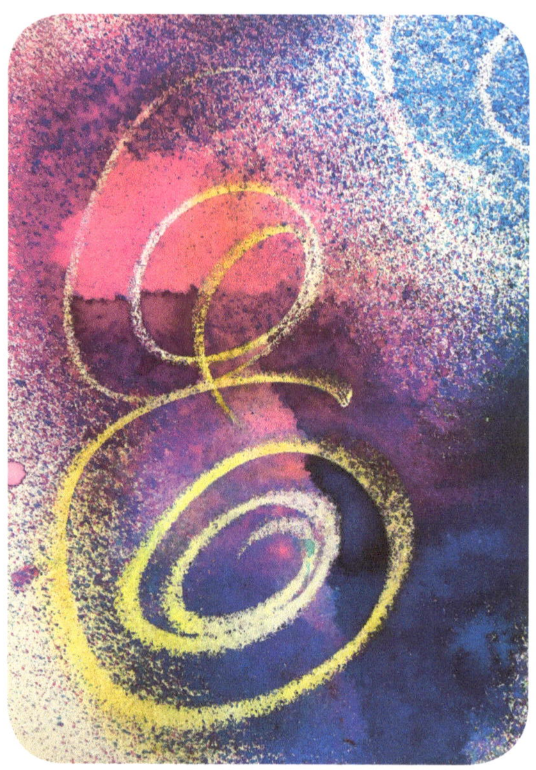

Yellow chalk pastel fills in a white mark left behind by using cras pas resist on an ink-sprayed page.

of your stamps regularly, as it can clog any fine areas in the stamp. (I clean my stamps with baby wipes.) I usually work with pigment inks when I want to create a bit of design or pattern as a top layer. I tend to purchase pigment ink in black or metallic to provide a contrasting top layer. There are many brands of pigment inkpads, my favorites are Momento, Versamark or ColorBox.

Dye inkpads have ink that is not tacky or

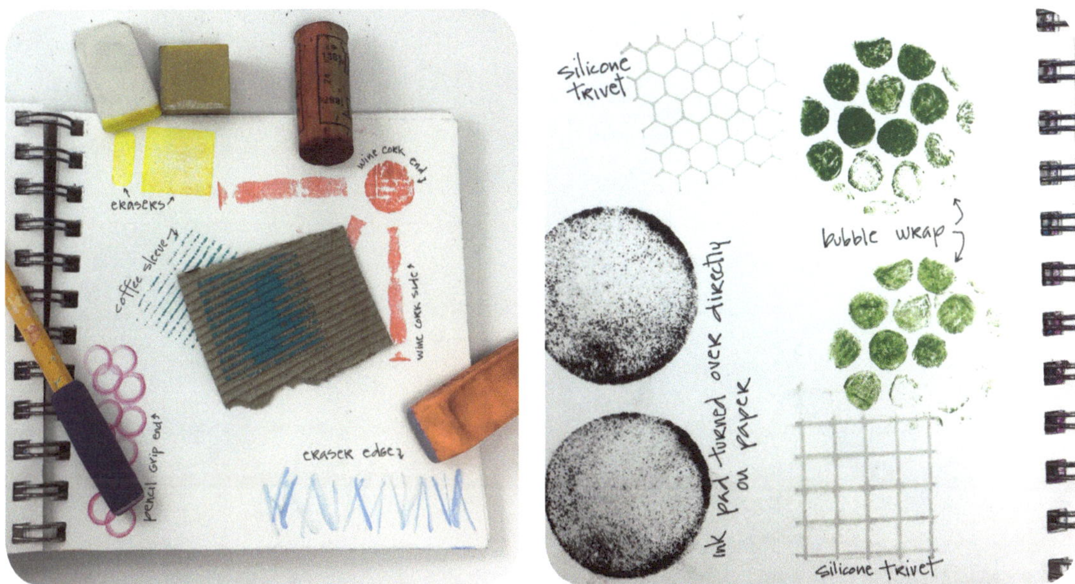

The search for "found" stamps will put you right in the middle of the "what if" mind frame. A variety of household items can be put to work as stamps—from erasers to bubble wrap. A test page or two in your art journal will help you track your discoveries.

sticky. Dye ink is not necessarily permanent. There are a full range of colors and intensities and many brands to choose from. Some say water "washable" on the box, some just say "kids" ink (assuming it will wash off their skin). Since dye inks may bleed when exposed to water, they, too, can be used for the top layer easily; just be aware that any wet application that goes on top of this stamp ink might cause it to bleed.

Distress inkpads contain a hybrid ink that is most closely related to dye ink. However, the Distress ink (this is a brand name, made by Ranger products, not a description of what happens to the paper or the artist) is meant to be water-reactive so you can count on any wet media causing it to blur, get runny and create a watercolor effect. I love these inks because the inkpad sits up a bit, allowing you to turn the pad upside down and press it directly onto your page (eliminating a need for rubber stamps). You can scrape it along the edge of your page for a border or frame effect. You can also swipe a paint brush wet with clean water over the ink mark to purposely bleed areas. These inks are so versatile; I usually take one or two colors with me to use while traveling even though

I try to keep my supplies to a minimum when on the road.

Considering all three types of inkpads, I suggest only investing in one or two pigment inkpads (black and copper) and as many of the Distress inks as you want to keep on hand.

Stamping in the Zone

Here we are again at another "what if" moment. Remember that wine cork I found on my desk? What if I use the round end in place of a rubber stamp? Cool shapes!

After the cork discovery, I started looking around for other patterned or random things to use as stamps in otherwise non-art-supply drawers. I discovered a few silicone hot pads (with the little checkerboard patterns on them) that I could cut up. Most students have tried bubble wrap stamps: totally fun, too! Even something as simple as a pencil eraser makes lovely marks, as will foam pencil grips.

Collage Collaborations

Now let's find a way to use your practice pages as collage material and get them into your art journal.

Once you have applied chalk in some areas on the practice pages (either an India ink page or a Dylusion page), find some visually interesting areas on the page and cut them into circles

(discs), squares, rectangles and leaves following the instructions below. (Be sure to save any additional scraps from cutting your practice pages for future collage work in your journal.)

Creating Circles (Discs)

1. Place a roll of masking tape (or any other circular shape you can see through) onto various areas on the practice paper.
2. Move the masking tape around looking for circular areas that somehow speak to you.

We don't have to get too academic here: Sure, you might be drawn to areas with the most contrast of shapes and darks and lights, but you can really just let go and embrace an intuitive approach.

3. As you find interesting areas inside the masking tape circle, use a pencil to trace the circle and then cut it out with scissors. These discs will become full of their own personality. I guarantee you will find shapes and areas you love even if you were not thrilled with the full practice page when you viewed it as a singular piece.

Cutting squares, rectangles, leaves

1. Cut out six small squares (about 1 inch by 1 inch) from random places on your practice pages.
2. Cut out a rectangle shape (approximately

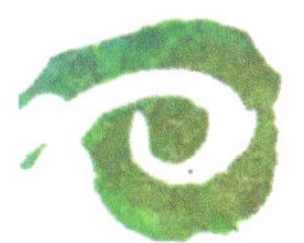

Stamps as Layers

Here is the magic; the stamped image may be either a first layer (used on the white page) or added on top of other techniques already applied to the page. Rubber stamps (with dye, Distress or pigment ink) work well applied over ink sprays and chalks, especially if there is an area on your page that is not bringing you complete joy and feels like it needs something else. But stamps can also do a great job preparing a page. I invite you to try a few more page preps in your journal:

- Try creating a repeating border with your stamps going around the sides of a page.

- Apply a stamp design over the entire page, then apply some chalk over the stamps to see how they collaborate.

- Apply a stamp design over the entire page, then apply some Dylusions spray inks over the stamps to see what happens.

- Apply your stamp designs over some India ink blooms on a journal page.

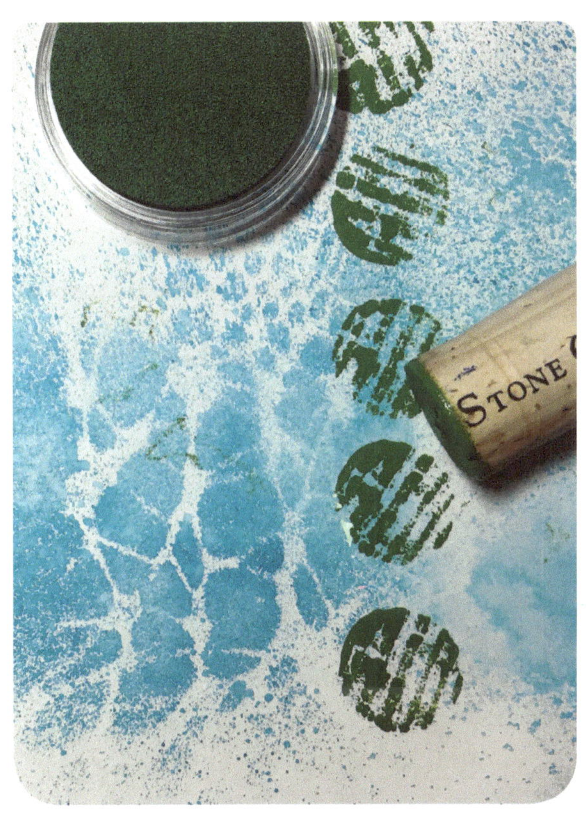

2 by 4 inches, but any size will do) that will fit on your journal page.

3. Cut out a few simple leaf shapes.

Working with the circles

Glue one of the cut circular shapes onto a page in your journal that has been prepared with any of the techniques described in the previous chapters, using a glue stick. When using glue sticks, be sure to spread the glue evenly over the entire back surface of the shape. You can work on top of scrap paper (like old catalogs or magazines) to catch the glue as you go over the edges of the shape, making sure that there are no spots that remain without glue. Then apply your glued shape to the page and rub the entire surface, making sure that all the glue comes in contact with the surface you want it to stick to. Rubbing ensures there are no air bubbles that will cause the glue to dry and the shape to pop off later. Using this method allows you to get great results with any glue stick on the market; no need to spend additional money on brand names. The only glue sticks not to use are those labeled "re-positional" as they just don't have the same sticking power as regular, or permanent, glue sticks, regardless of brand.

Now that you have one of the discs glued

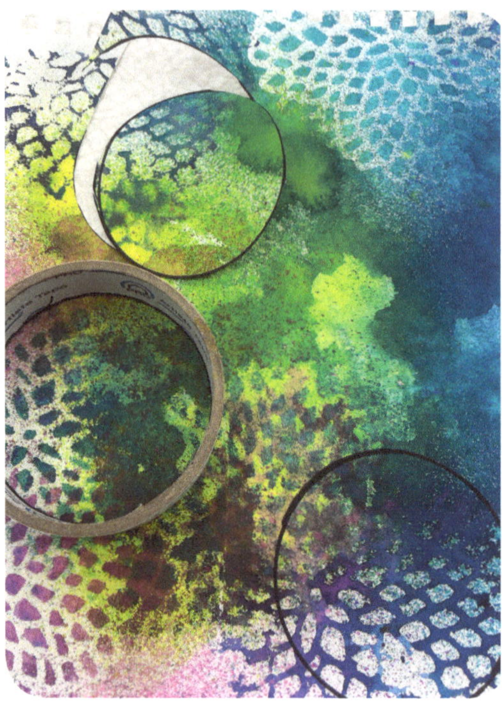

Trace the inside of a roll of masking tape to create circle shapes on your practice pages. Then cut the circles out to use as collage items in your art journal.

down, you can explore some what-ifs. What if you add text going around the circle? Or add chalk to the rest of the page? You can rubber stamp designs on to the disc and the surrounding page. Or do it all (chalk, handwriting, stamps): The sky is the limit! You can even add some decorative tape to the top of the glued disc or around the page as a border.

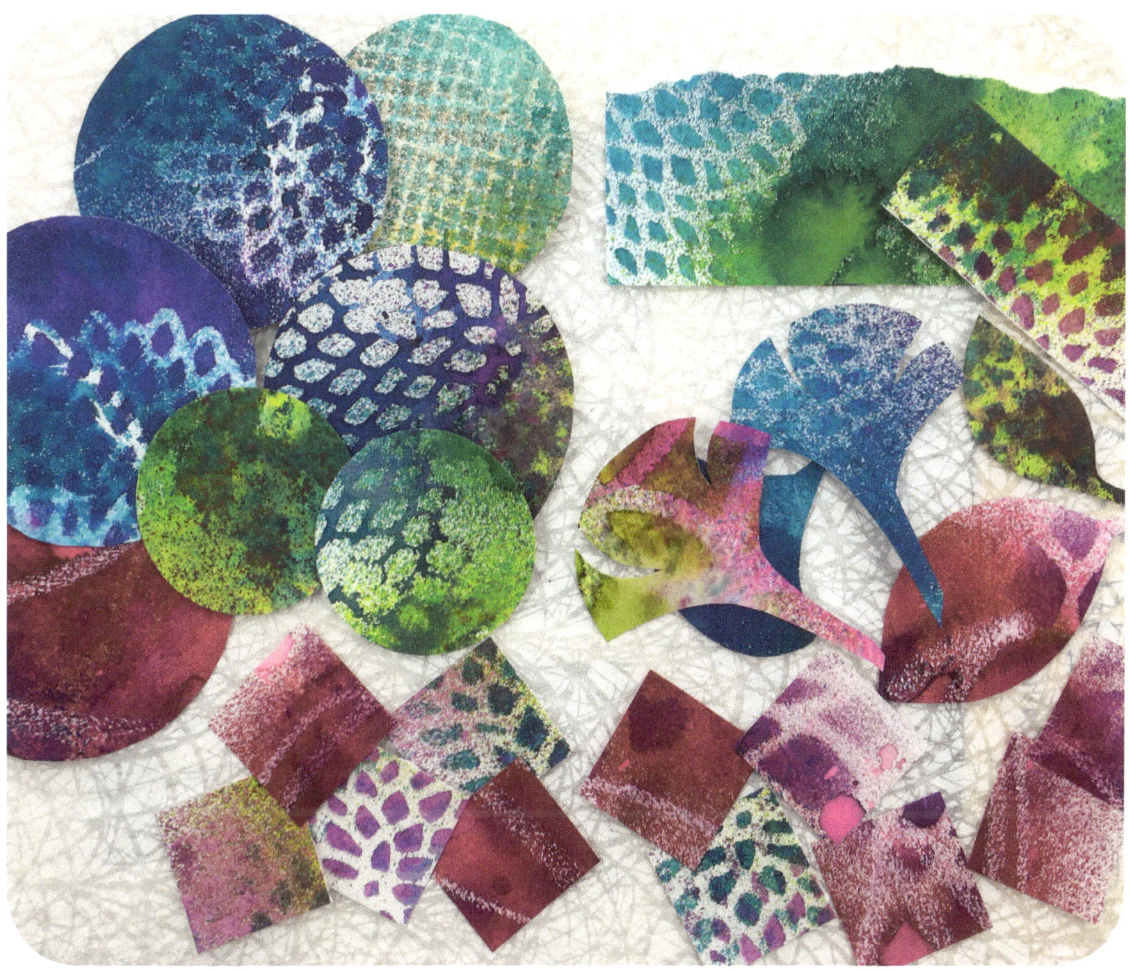

Practice pages work perfectly as collage fodder. Cut or tear a variety of shapes to bring another layer of visual and tactile interest to your art journal.

The disc starts the page and you can play with additional layers to finish the page to your satisfaction.

Here is another way to attach a disc on the same page or on another prepared page in your book. You will use a decorative brad (fastener) instead of glue, which will allow the disc to be moved like a spinner, creating an interactive element in your art journal.

To attach the disc with a decorative fastener or brad:

1. Use a pushpin to punch a hole first in the middle of the disc, then in the journal page where you would like the disc to be attached. If you are feeling really adventurous, you can even attach this disc so part of it hangs off the page and sticks out from the side of the book.

2. Then insert the fastener through both the disc and the page.

3. Open the wings of the fastener on the back of the page so it stays in place but can spin.

4. To add a bit of fun, create a little tab on the disc by sticking one end of a piece of decorative tape to the front of the disc, then fold the tape in half and stick the other end to the back of the disc. The tape becomes a tab that you can use to turn the disc.

A great journal prompt for personal writing inspired by the disc is musing on the notion of "never-ending conversations." I find it an interesting process to write about these conversations going in a circle around the disc, or hidden entirely under the disc. Never-ending conversations can be wonderful (like those I have with my sister) or nerve wracking (like self-talk that is not always beneficial).

Working with the squares

I love grids, they are surprisingly interesting when used on your journal page. Put the 1-inch squares into a grid formation by lining

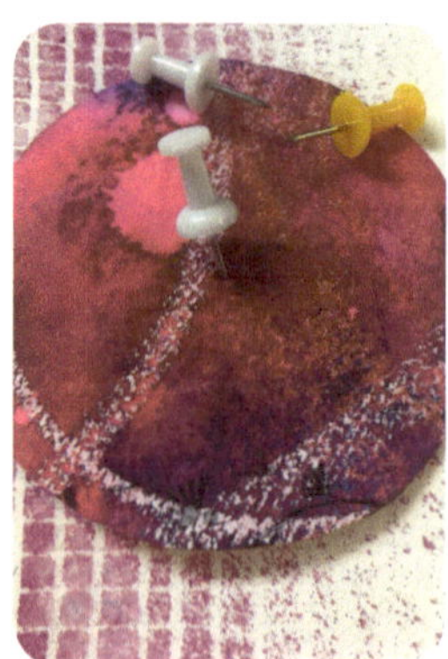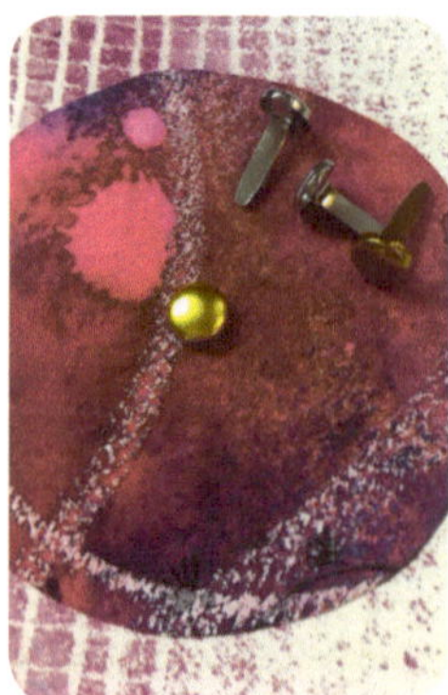

Use a push pin, thumbtack or book awl to make a hole in a circle and your journal page. Attach the circle with a brad so it can spin freely.

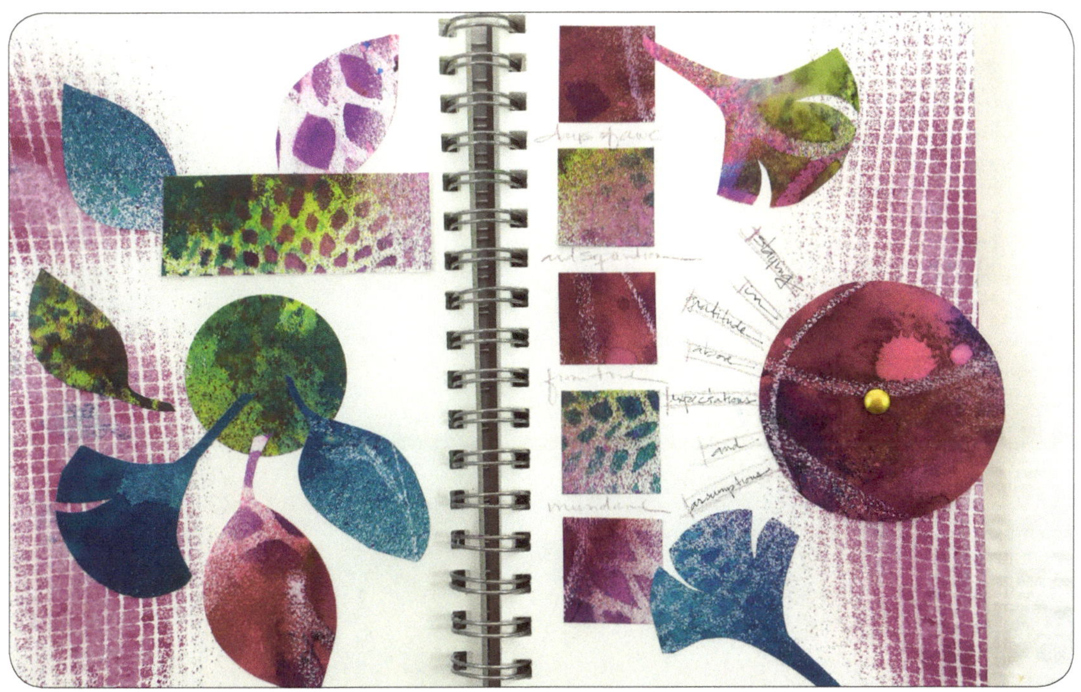

Shapes cut from practice pages are collaged on to a journal spread. A spinning disc adds an interactive element to the page on the right.

them up three across in two rows. Be sure to leave some space between each square so there is room for some handwriting in those areas.

After doing some journal writing in the lines between the squares, you can add some chalk applied with a cotton square over the text. Do you see how the layers add interest on each page?

Leaves

Leaf shapes (cut from your practice pages) are great collage additions to any page in your journal especially if you can vary the size of the leaves. If you glue them on top of a prepared page you will be adding a second layer. If they need a little "punch" to stand out, try coloring just the edge of the leaf with either chalk (applied with a cotton square) or rubber stamp ink.

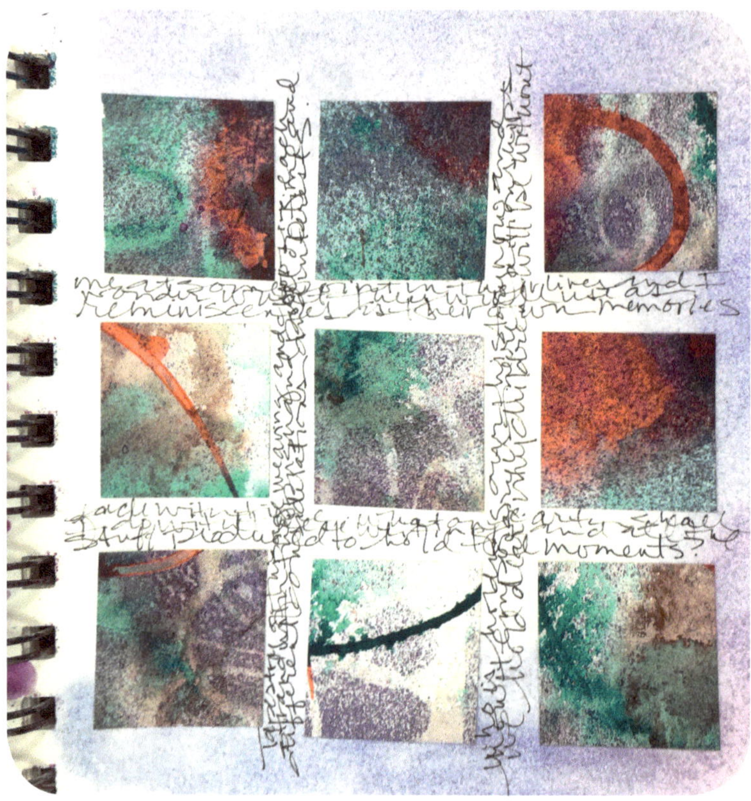

Feeling a bit stuck? Try attaching squares in a grid pattern to your page with a glue stick. The horizontal and vertical lines that appear between the squares are perfect for writing a journal entry.

Journal Prompt

The spaces that are created by the grid (in between the squares) call out to me for some handwriting. The horizontal and vertical lines intersect; like woven areas. A journal prompt for this page could be:

> *What is being woven into your life right now?*

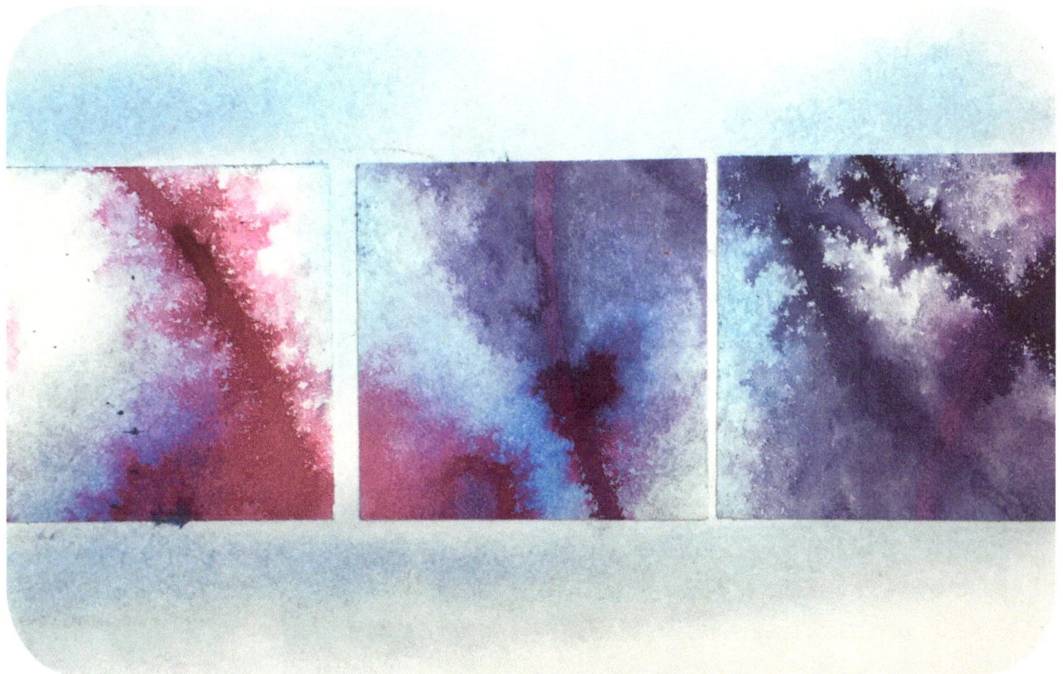

If a portion of a practice page lacks appeal, try cutting it into smaller shapes and arranging them on a journal page. These squares were highlighted with a smudgy chalk outline.

Rectangles

I love interactive elements as they engage me in a unique way when I add them to a page. The rectangle you cut out is easy to attach as a sleeve holder for a tag or a special piece of paper that you want to include on a journal page. You may decide to put these elements directly on top of the prepared pages that have chalk, ink or rubber stamps already applied as layers. Or you may prefer to work on a blank page using the interactive process to help encourage your creative expression.

1. Hold the rectangle horizontally across your page, being sure it will fit between the edges of your page.

2. Add a line of glue along the right and left edge, only about ½ inch wide (don't put any glue in the middle section of the rectangle).

3. Attach the paper rectangle to your page, rubbing over the glued areas on the right and left sides to be sure they stick.

4. The middle section of the rectangle will not have any glue, so a piece of paper (or a tag) can slide behind the rectangle sleeve.

Flap or door

All you need to create a door or flap on a page is a piece of paper smaller than your journal page (squares or rectangles work best) and some decorative tape. The paper for your flap should be a bit stiff; I like to work with either card stock or a piece of the practice paper scraps I saved from exploring the ink spray techniques in chapters 4 and 5. If you wish to use some collage paper (or a map) that is a bit thin, you can always glue two pieces of paper together using a glue stick.

1. Cut the flap to a size that is smaller than your full journal page.
2. Attach a piece of washi tape to one side of the rectangle which will become the flap: half the tape should be on the flap and half the tape should hang off the flap. (I suggest running the tape vertically along the entire left side.)
3. Trim the tape so it is the exact same height of the flap (both top and bottom edge of the tape should be even with the top and bottom of the flap).
4. Set the flap down on your art journal page and rub the part of the tape that is hanging off of the flap onto the page.
5. Your flap (or door) should swing open and shut easily.
6. Optional: Add a little tab of paper or tape on the opposite side of the flap to make it easier to grasp as you swing the door open and shut.
7. What if...? There are tons of variations to explore with this one technique.

I often use a flap or door in my travel journal. It is a great way to add a business card or another piece of ephemera that I might have picked up in my wanderings to a journal page. This method of attachment also allows you to see both the front and back of the card or paper, giving you another surface to enjoy.

Pocket

Here is yet another way to use a piece of that practice paper we created earlier or a section of a map or other interesting piece of paper. There is something about a pocket that calls for curiosity and action. What might be in there?

To create a pocket all you have to do is cut a shape you can fit onto your journal page. Another rectangle will work well, but any shape will do (even a heart or leaf).

1. Apply glue to three sides of the pocket; both right and left and then bottom.
2. Place the pocket down on your page and rub over the glue to be sure there is

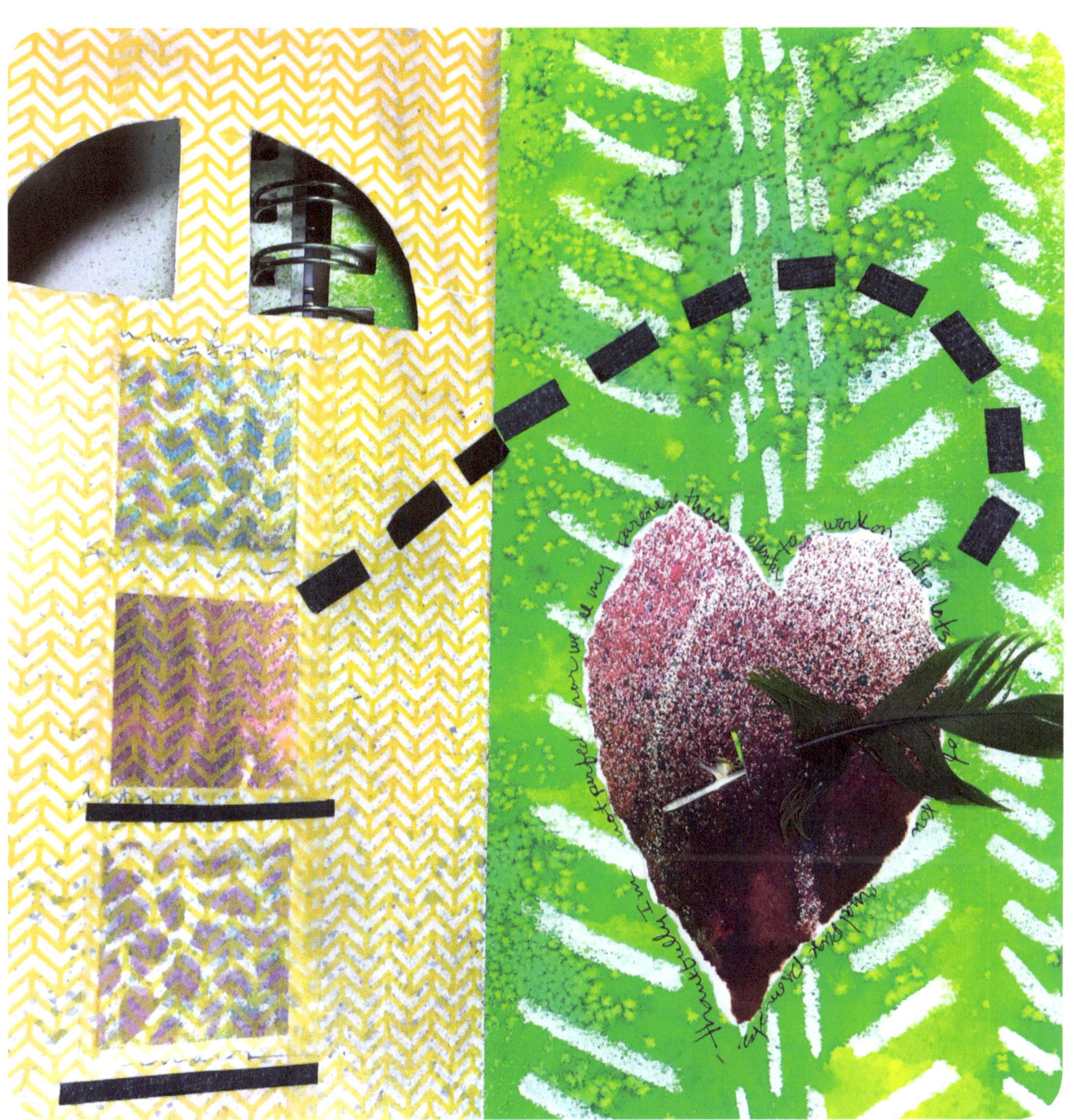

This door-like flap that I taped to a journal page can be opened to reveal the collaged heart and feather tucked behind it.

good contact between the journal page and your cut shape.

3. You now have a pocket glued down.

What will you put in the pocket?

I love to slip shipping tags into my journal pockets. Office supply stores often sell these tags with either string or wire hanging from the holes in the end. Large craft stores sell them as well as fine paper stores that sell wrapping paper and supplies.

Photos work beautifully in the pockets, especially the old printed or Polaroid photos on stiff paper. Have a favorite quote? It is lovely to find it written on a piece of paper in the pocket. Or tuck away a treasured letter or postcard.

A sleeve is the same as a pocket with one difference. It is glued on just the two opposite sides, usually along the full right and left sides.

An alternative attachment option for a pocket or sleeve is to use decorative washi tape in place of glue stick. The tape adds another visual element on the page. Once I have the tape in my hands I often apply it more as decoration than just something functional. I have used the washi tape to make flower stems, to create borders on empty pages, to obscure my stream of conscious writing in places or to create arrows. I have used decorative tape to clean up the back of the door or flap if the underside needs a little attention. I have even applied tape to the

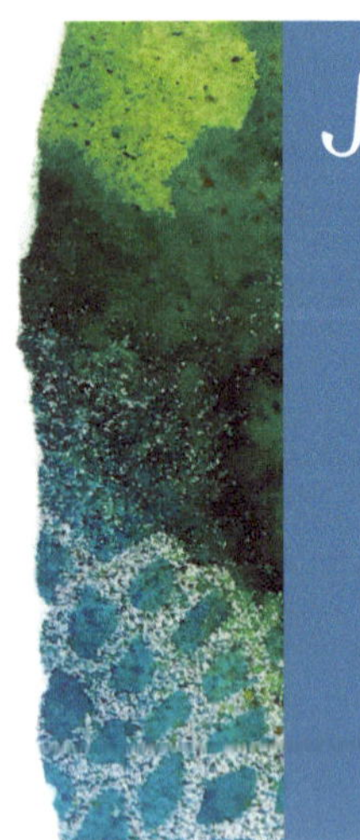

Journal Prompt

Interactive elements invite directed journal writing prompts:

> *What doors do you wish would open in your world?*

> *What keeps certain doors closed?*

> *What do you wish you could see out your front door?*

> *How do we lock our front doors?*

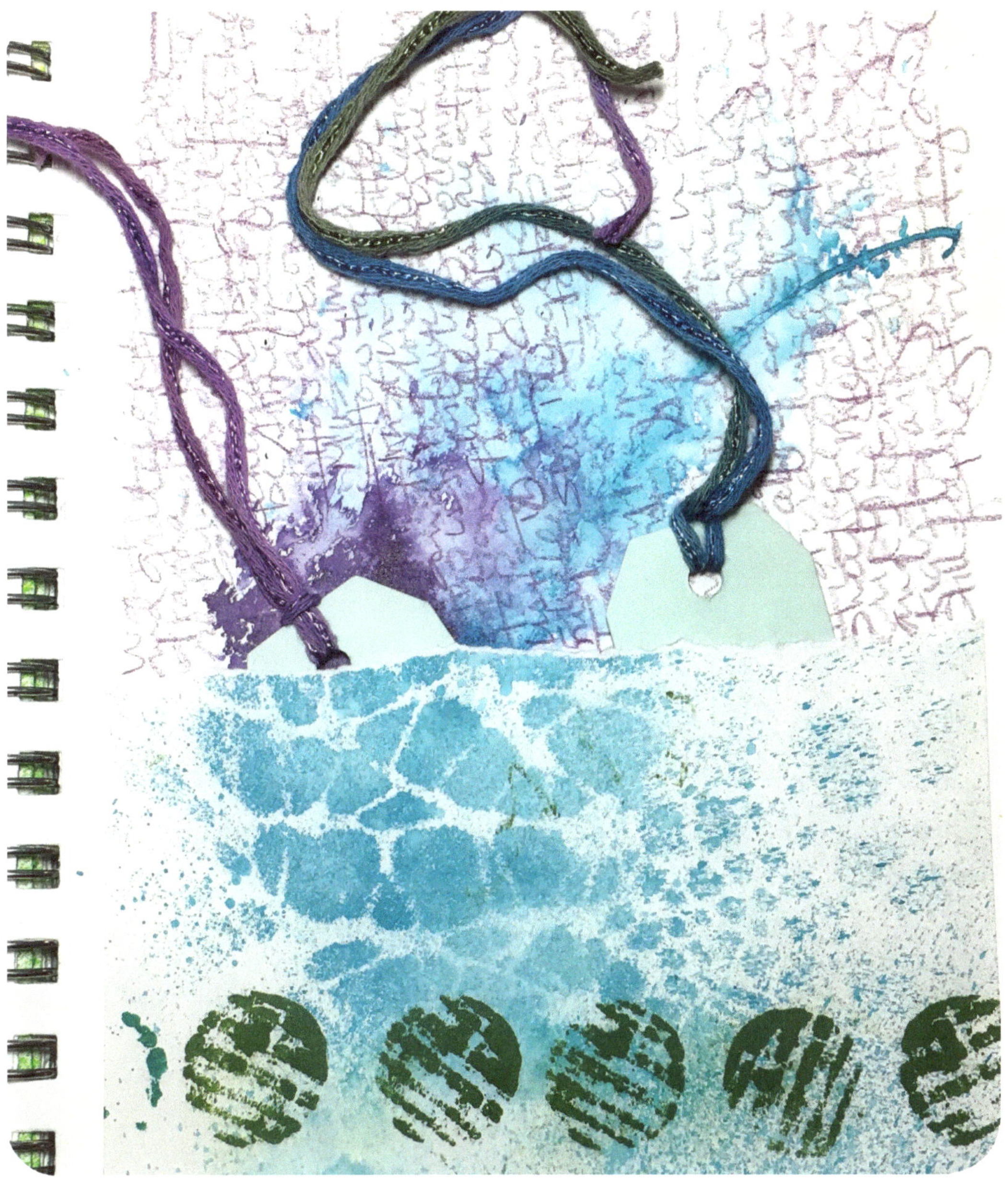

Gluing three sides of a torn rectangle to the page creates a pocket that's perfect for holding tags, photos or treasured bits of paper.

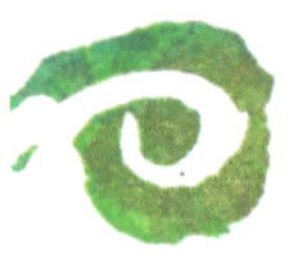# What If You Need a Do-over?

As I review my work, I become aware that there are pages that just don't satisfy me. While this is a book about joyful pages, the reality of the journal practice (or any art practice) is that times of joy are occasionally accompanied by the reverse response.

Yes, it is true. We have to honor the dissatisfaction, the uncomfortable times and the struggles to create layers of beauty that come up short. I call it the black hole; where nothing I am adding to the page is making it joyous or even decent. The grand "ugh."

Every artist, every art journaler, every "creative" has experienced this time of stuckness. But there is hope and an easy fix, a "reset button" you can use.

1. Lay open your art journal so it is flat and simply paint a thin coat of white gesso on top of the offending (or uninspiring, boring or horrible) page. (Be sure to wash your brush as soon as you finish painting. If you let the gesso dry on the brush it will ruin the bristles.)

2. The gesso will go on as an opaque layer, but as it dries it becomes fairly transparent, allowing the bottom layers to "glow" through the white paint. You can see an example in the photos at right.

3. Once the gesso dries, it may be left alone to add a quiet, blended layer on top of a busy page. Or you can add color once again. The surface of the dried gesso will be absorbent and slightly rough. It will accept India ink or the Dylusion spray (taking a little longer to dry than when you apply these to the raw paper) and chalk will stick on the gesso when applied with a piece of cotton.

front of my art journal to add a personal touch if the cover is plain.

All of the techniques we have explored (India ink, Dylusions ink, chalk, rubber stamps) work well together and may be layered up in any order. These are great collaborators and complement each other. If your first layer (any technique) is not bringing you complete and utter joy, then try adding another layer on top. When in doubt, keep going!

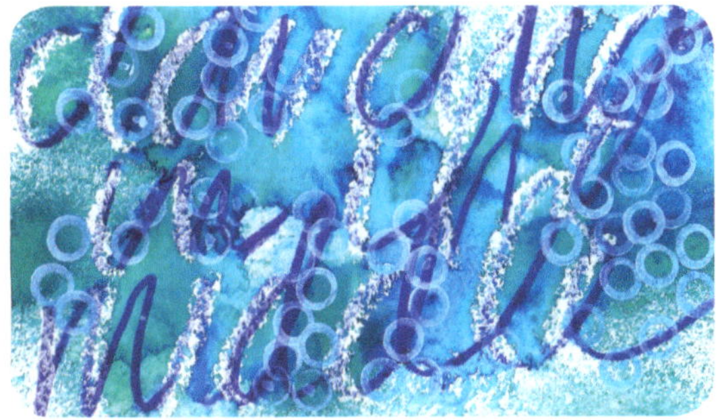

This page just did not seem to work even with the layers of text, crayon resist and spray inks. It just was not a joyful page for me.

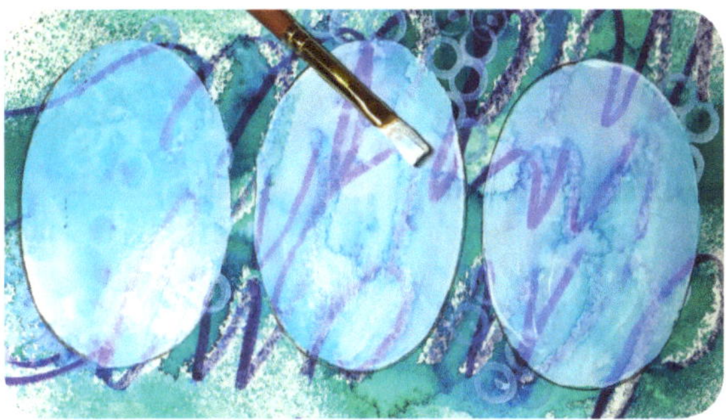

Instead of ripping the page out of my art journal, I decided to trace around an oval shape, then paint the shapes with a thin layer of white gesso—my favorite "do over" material.

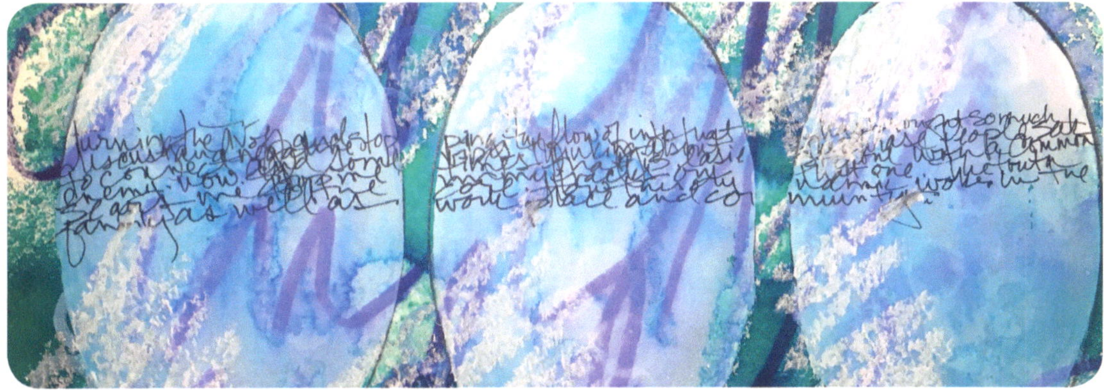

When the gesso was dry, I wrote a journal entry using a Micron pen directly on top of the gesso. I also applied white cray pas directly on top of the egg shapes and the writing. I now like the page better; the egg shapes seem to be floating with a bit of mystery.

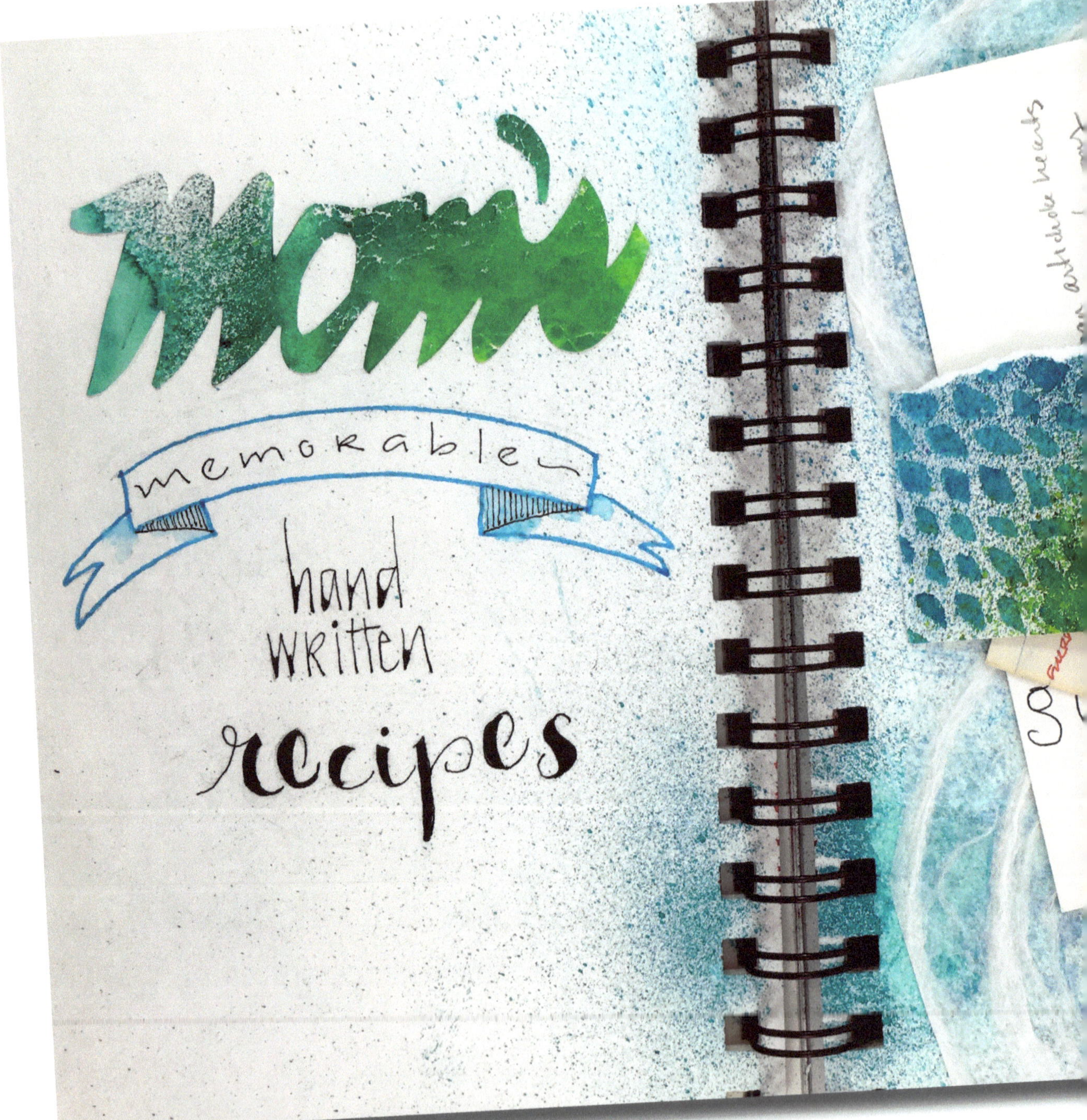

Mom's
memorable
hand
written
recipes

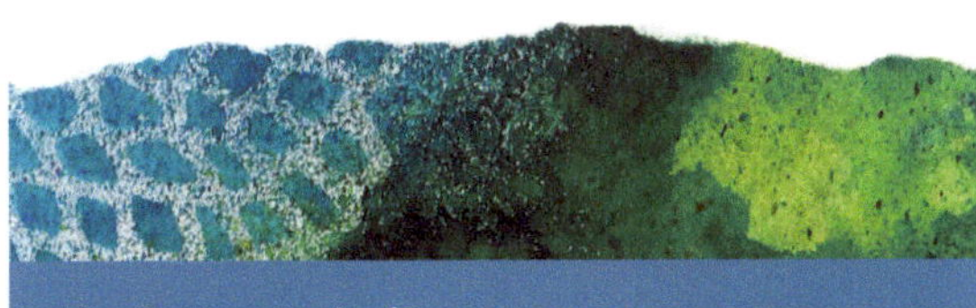

Journal Prompt

I found a recipe
in my mom's handwriting,
which I slipped behind a sleeve.
I love seeing her handwriting on
the paper being "hugged" to the
journal page.

> *Do you have a favorite poem or sentimental piece of paper that you can slide behind a rectangle sleeve or slip in a pocket?*

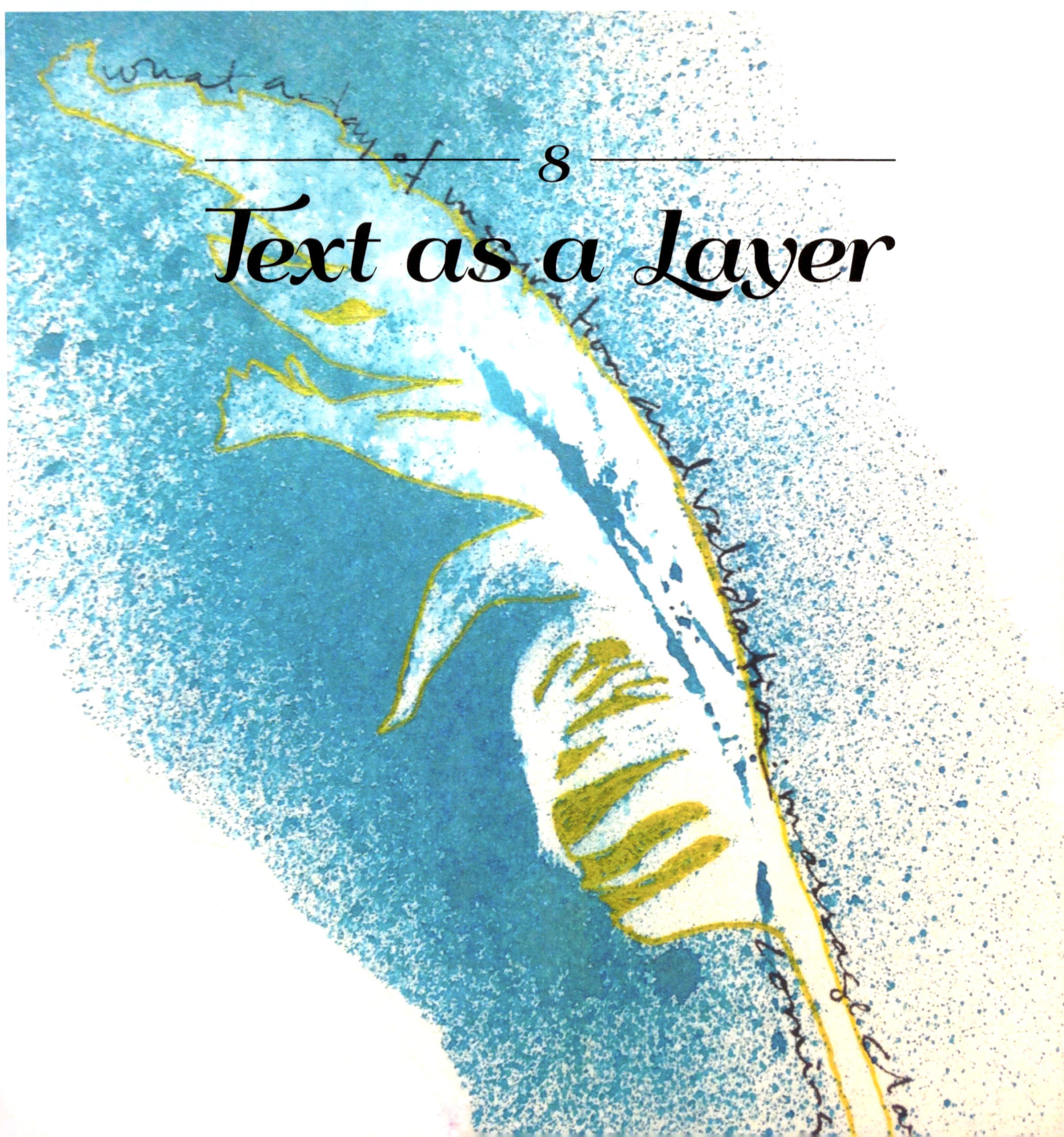

8

Text as a Layer

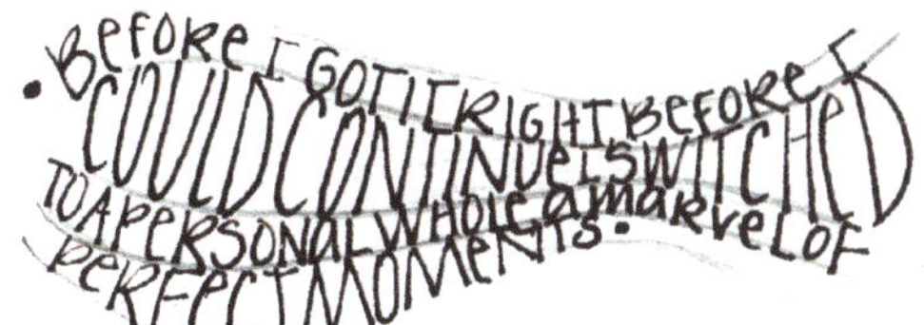

The use of text in art journaling often becomes an emotionally loaded subject. I have observed students stiffen up with the suggestion to add text, and I have seen students go the exact opposite route and spend most of the workshop pouring out their thoughts on their prepared pages. The most important consideration is: Where are you right now, and what will feel most meaningful? Finding joy in art journaling means that our creative expression is grounded in where we are right now. Taking away all the shoulds will remind us that there are no rules and position us for the creative freedom that will lead us into the zone.

Text as the First Layer

Let's start by taking a look at using text as a graphic element and first layer, keeping in mind we intend to add layers on top of the writing.

Letters (text) are basically linear marks that form a pattern on the page.

Materials

BASICS
- **Your art journal**

FOCUS MATERIALS FOR THIS CHAPTER
- **A discarded page from an old book (or a photocopy of a page from an old book)**
- **A Tombow Dual Brush water-based pen, pick a color that blends well with your India ink and Dylusion sprays**
- **A Pigma Brush pen with permanent ink (I prefer the Sakura brand pens)**
- **A Sakura Micron Pen #005 (permanent ink, tiny tip)**
- **Dylusions spray ink**
- **India ink**
- **Nitrile gloves**
- **Apron**
- **Wax paper**
- **Paper towels**
- **Glue stick**
- **Set of chalk pastels**
- **White cray pas oil pastel**
- **Small spray bottle**
- **Commercial stencil (or found object mask)**
- **Pencil with eraser**

Imagine looking at a page of writing in a language you don't understand, where you can't pick out different letterforms. We typically see the patterns in isolation; thick and thin lines, curves and angles, space that gets filled either horizontally or vertically. Some lines might rise up above other marks, some shapes dip down below.

Now imagine that we are going to use our writing in the same, graphic manner. For this exercise, the actual word meanings are not as important as the word shapes, so go ahead and take the pressure off. You don't have to find the most profound, personally meaningful words for this first layer since we will cover the text with additional layers. Settle on a quote you have in your head, a slogan from an advertisement or a headline from today's news feed.

Are you hearing voices in your head criticizing your own, personal handwriting? Please invite these darlings to leave the room and find something to do for a bit. You don't need to worry about any handwriting issues; the text will be covered with a second layer, and this is about journaling in the zone, not journaling with your inner critics screaming for attention.

To create a first layer of text, we are going to experiment with two different types of pen-brushes. The first is a water-reactive mark made with a Tombow (or similar) brush pen, which means that it will bleed and move when water is applied, the second page will explore permanent marks made with a black brush pen.

Playtime

1. Open your journal to a blank page. (So far so good?)
2. Using the brush end of the Tombow, write the quote (or phrase you have chosen) using large, loopy cursive. It is OK if there is not enough room for the whole quote. It is cool to run the quote off the page so go right up to the edges.
3. On part of the page, set down a commercial stencil or found object mask and spray a light mist of Dylusion spray over part of your writing. Watch how the pigment from the Tombow will pick up and bleed a bit. Have a paper towel handy to blot any puddles.
4. Next, spray a little bit of clean water on the rest of the Tombow writing, then drip a little India ink into the wet surfaces creating the ink bloom we learned about in chapter 4. Again, be prepared to blot any puddles.
5. Remember to use the nitrile gloves when

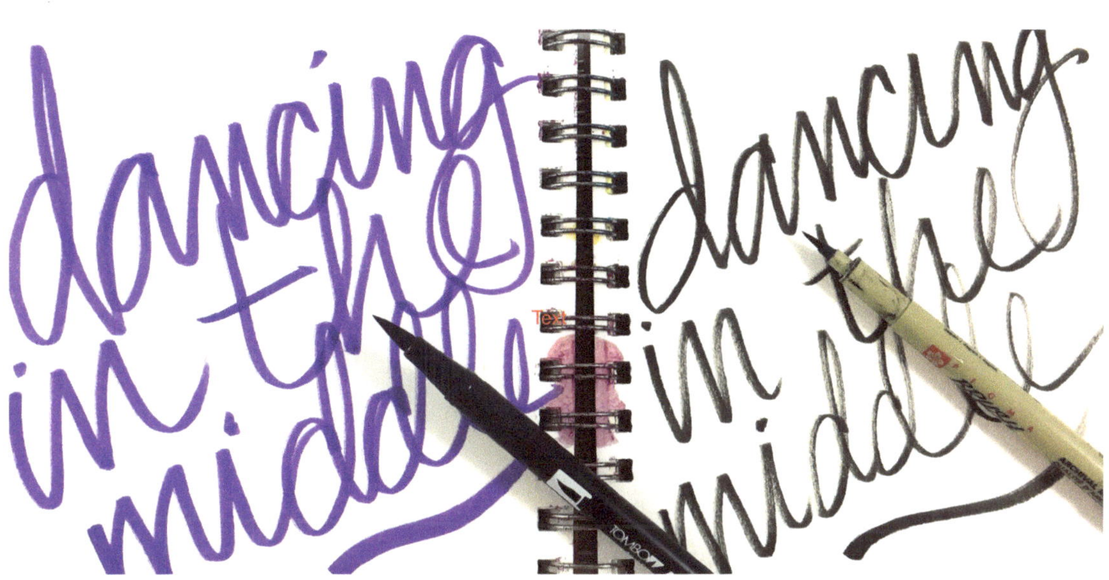

Try writing a few words in both a water-reactive pen and a permanent ink pen in large loopy letters.

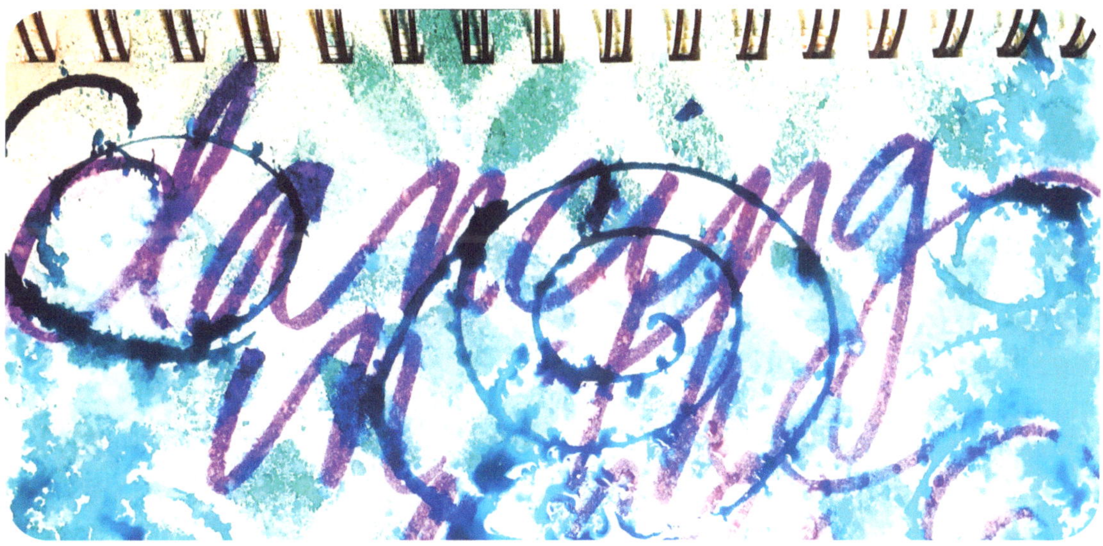

Spray ink over the letters with a stencil or mask, then add a swirl of ink you can spritz with water to bloom on top of your writing.

working with the Dylusions sprays or India inks. Wearing an apron is advised and your work surface should be covered. When spraying ink directly onto a journal page in your book you might wish to put a piece of wax paper (or paper towels) behind the page you are spraying to keep the color from finding the other pages.

While we let this page dry you can pat yourself on the back for actually using your own handwriting without self-criticism. Did you notice that writing slowly, trying to make large and loopy shaped letters gets you in the flow of the moment? Sometimes the biggest challenge is the slow writing itself. Then spraying over the text makes magic by blurring, bleeding and blending the lines to create a layered, textured page.

Adding cray pas resist

1. On a new page, write the same phrase in the same manner (large and loopy) with a Tombow marker.

2. Then go over part of the Tombow marks with a white cray pas. Remember to press the crayon down hard as you write.

3. Now add one of the wet techniques you just tried above; either the Dylusions spray ink or the water and India ink blooms.

The cray pas will create the resist and keep some of the Tombow marks from bleeding, other areas will run a bit. You are well on your way to creating luscious layers.

Working with a permanent pen

Once your pages have dried enough to be able to open your book to another blank page, repeat the experiment using text as the bottom layer, only this time, write your phrase using the black brush pen with per-

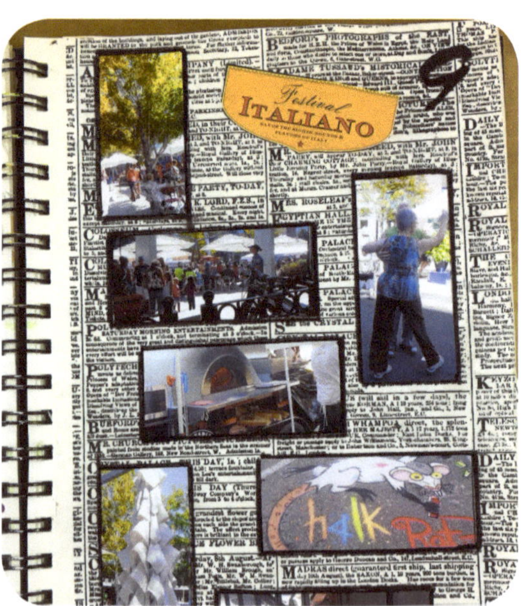

Joyce Breheny used photos, a label and pen outlining to help this page, with its book text background, capture fun memories.

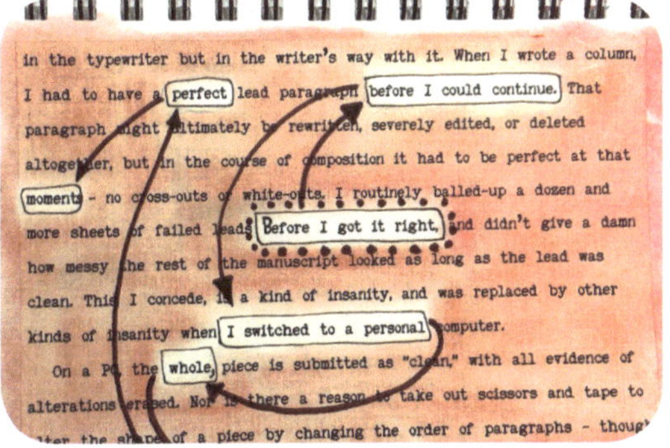

Glue a page pulled from an old or discarded book into your journal as a base layer on a page.

To create a "found" poem, rub chalk onto the book page, leaving words or phrases uncovered, then outline those words with a pen. Arrows can help guide the reading of the poem.

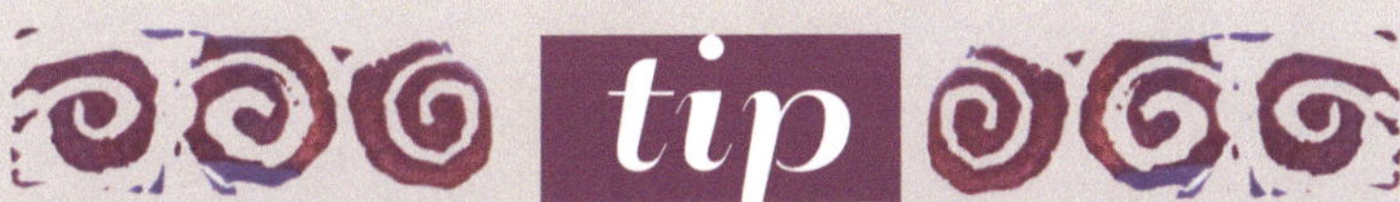

tip

Creating "found" poetry is a favorite pastime of mine. I love pulling random words from a page of discarded text and stringing them together to form a verse. This is a great way to get some original writing on a journal page. I typically use the words as the top layer; either highlighting them in glued down text or actually cutting out the words and carefully gluing them on top of a prepared page.

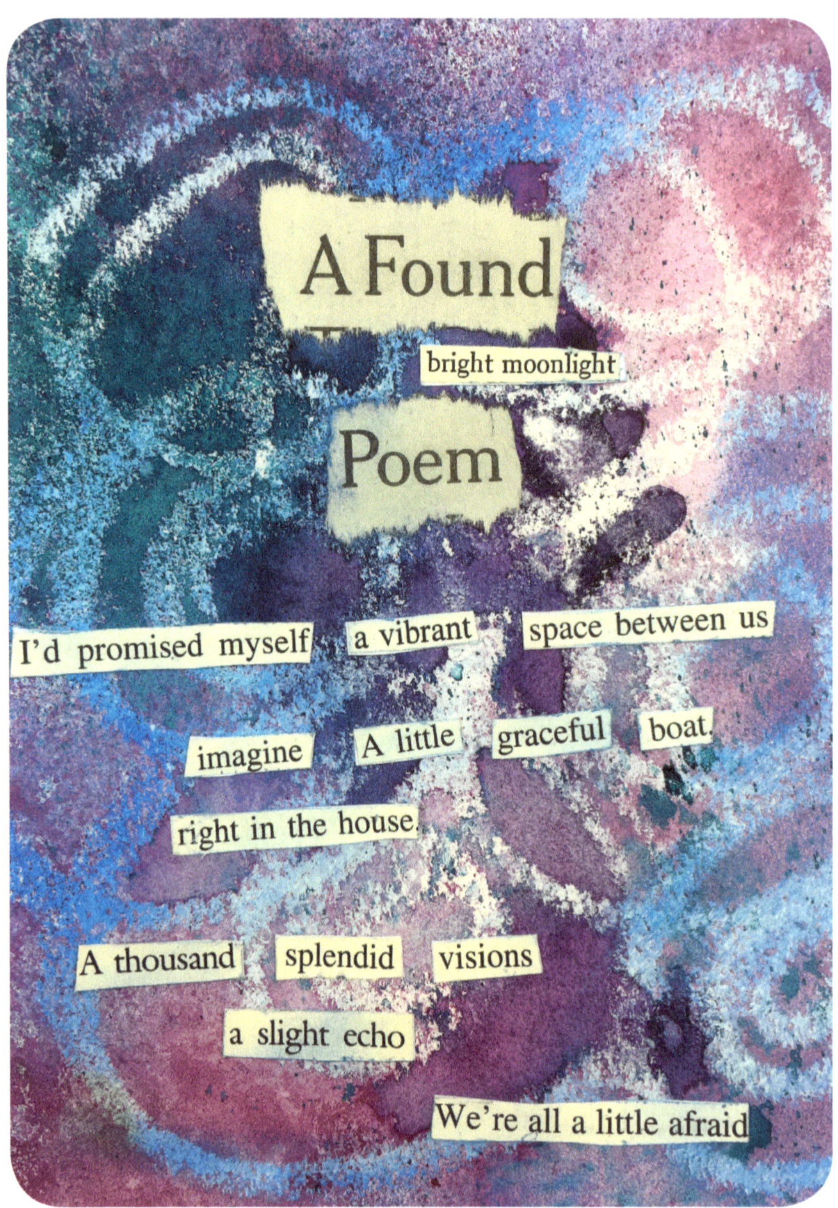

A "found" poem comes alive on a background of sprayed ink, chalk and cray pas resist.

manent ink. The pen marks won't move in water (give them a few minutes to dry completely before spraying any moisture on the text). Try this with the Dylusion spray ink, the India ink bloom, then the cray pas resist.

How do you like the build-up of layers? Have you asked "what if" as you completed these experiments? After the pages dry, what if you added chalk as a third layer? Now you are cooking!

Using book pages

One more way to work with text as a bottom layer that is guaranteed to give a satisfying result:

1. Cut a page from a discarded book or photocopy a page from a book that you don't wish to tear apart.

2. Glue the page onto a blank page in your journal with a glue stick.

3. Using a pencil, lightly circle some juicy phrases or words that you find randomly on the page.

4. Now try applying the chalk directly onto the text page, leaving the circled words alone (without chalk).

5. To highlight the words even more, you can circle them again with the permanent brush pen you used in the last exercise.

6. If you want the circled words to actually create a new phrase or "found" poem, add arrows from one word to the next, directing the eye to read them in order.

Text as a Top Layer

One of my earliest considerations when I started my art journal practice was dealing with the question about keeping my writing personal and judgment-free. I was concerned about the content (what if my kids read this stuff?) and the language (what if I misspelled a few words and my students read them?). I can still hear the laughter of the world directed at my abilities. I had to find a way to write freely; whether the content was dull and boring, or too personal, or just poorly written. I wanted to find a way to write freely because I found the writing to be a meditation, a cleansing, a way to process my life experiences. My answer was to find ways to obscure my writing and let go of the need to re-read most of my entries later. I invite you to try the techniques shown on page 101 for obscuring your writing, remembering to focus on the graphic elements that result. These techniques may be used as a first layer, although I seem to be most inspired to add writing to a prepared page.

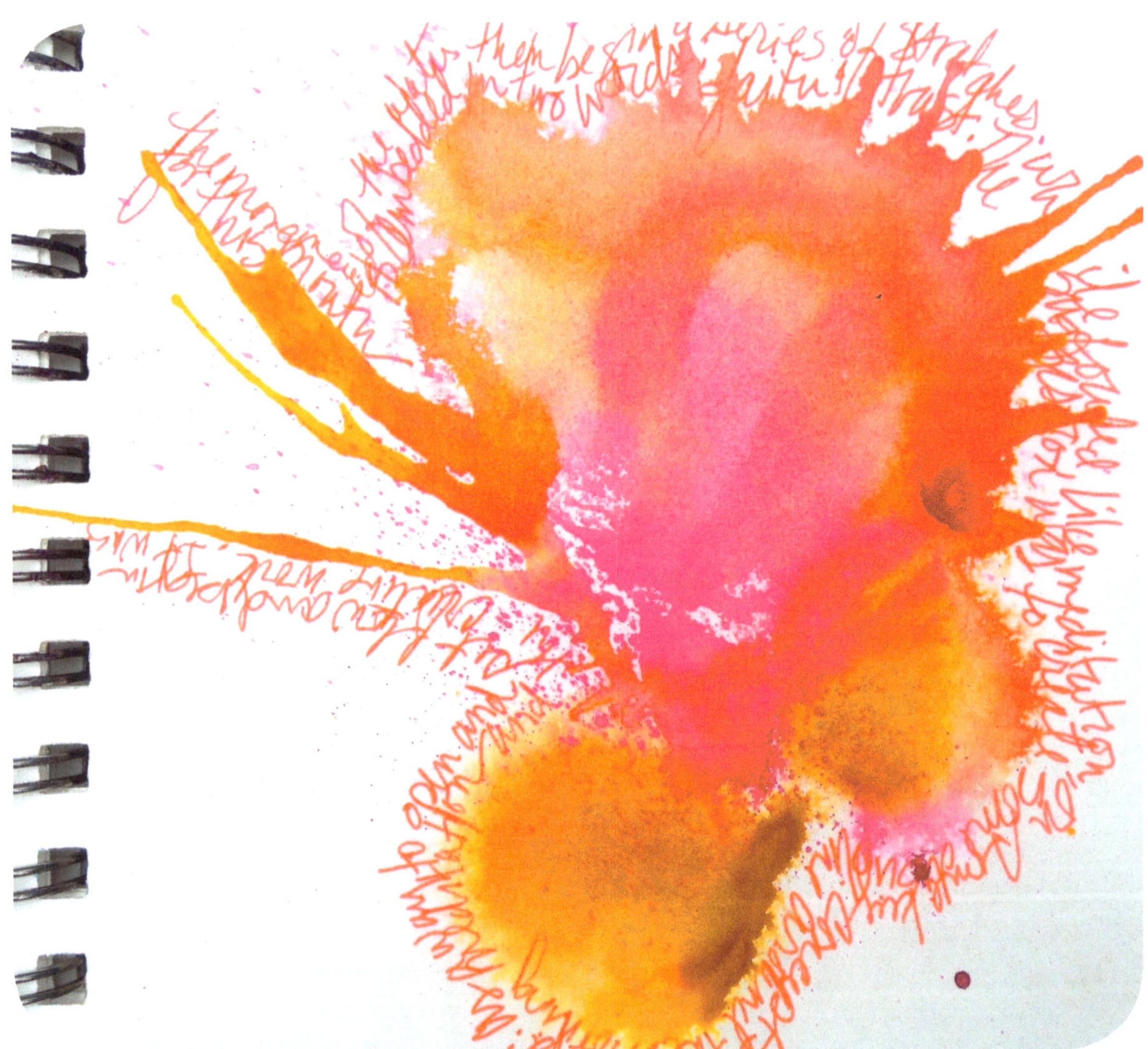

A sprayed bloom or splash can suggest areas for text; here I used a gel pen to write my thoughts around the edges of the shape.

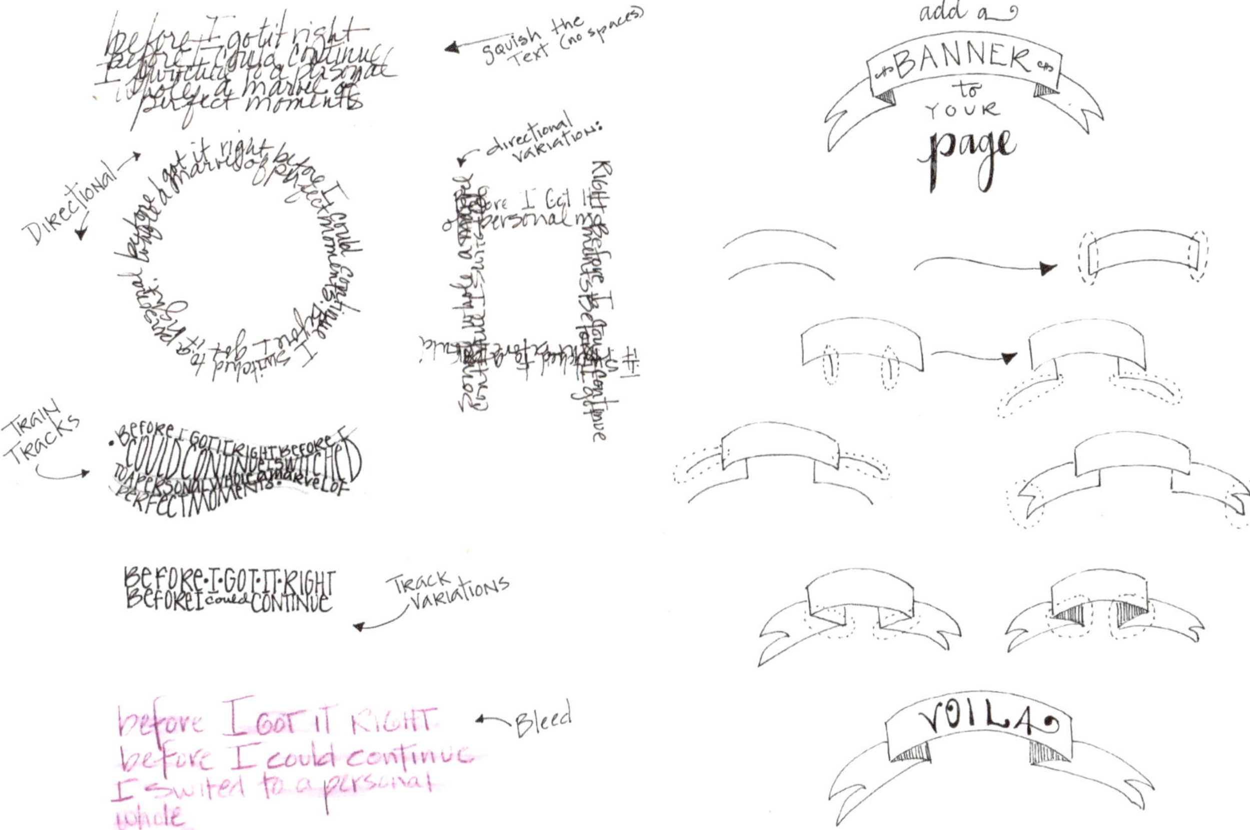

Handwritten text can also serve as a design element. Try one of these methods for obscuring handwriting so it can be used as a top layer.

Hand-drawn banners can make your text stand out on a colorful background.

Above, I offer a very simple step-by-step process for creating banners and little flourishes to punch out your text as a top layer. And I encourage you to continue to ask "what if" with your text efforts.

- What if I write in cursive with this thick pen?
- What if I write in tiny letters with this tiny tipped pen?
- What if I write a short entry with my non-dominant hand (yikes)?
- What if I write the entry with the Tombow pen then use a wet paintbrush to bleed just the edges?

Since writing is so personal, it is a good idea to figure out a few go-to techniques for including text in your journal that will bring you joy and allow you to get into the creative zone rather than adding stress. Remember there

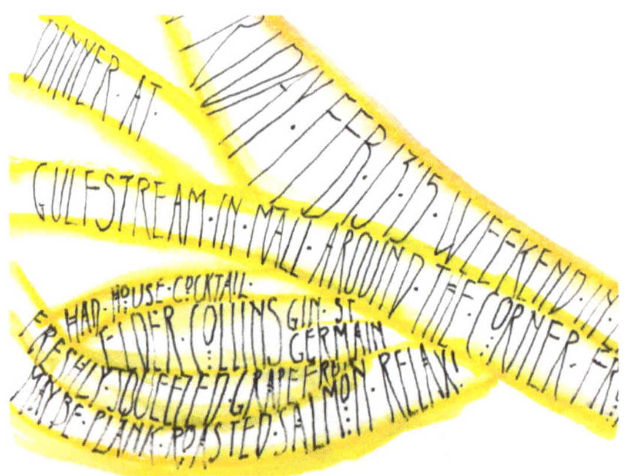

Create "train tracks" for writing by first making long, curvy, sometimes intersecting lines. Susie Coombe used red lines to create this train track style in her journal at right.

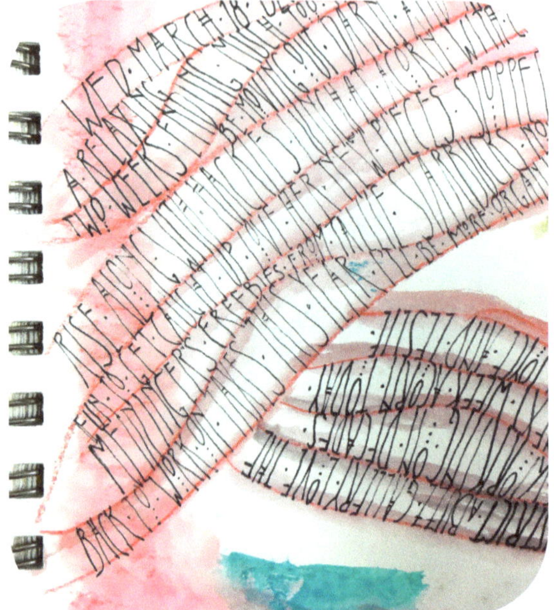

are no rules to art journaling. Give yourself permission to explore, erase, enjoy or ignore hand lettering. You may just find your groove by filling an art journal with favorite quotes.

If nothing else, creating a place to store your gratitude is a beautiful thing. If no words or text come to mind, make a list of all the things you are grateful for on a prepared page in your art journal, or create the list then work on top of it with techniques we covered earlier. It is a quick and satisfying way to add layers of both meaning and texture. What could be better?

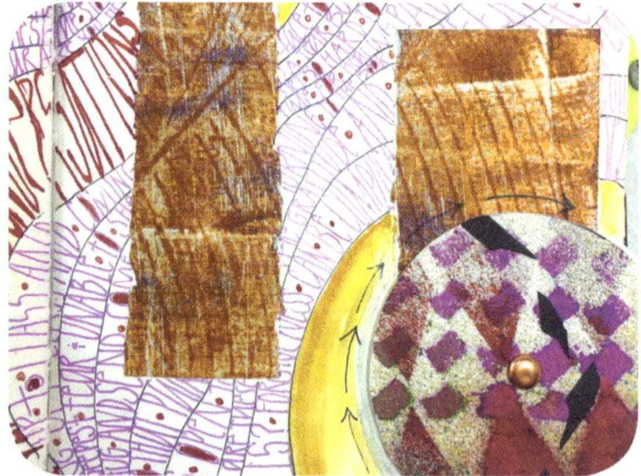

On this journal page, I attached a circle cut from a practice page with a decorative fastener in the center so it can turn. Text was added in the train tracks.

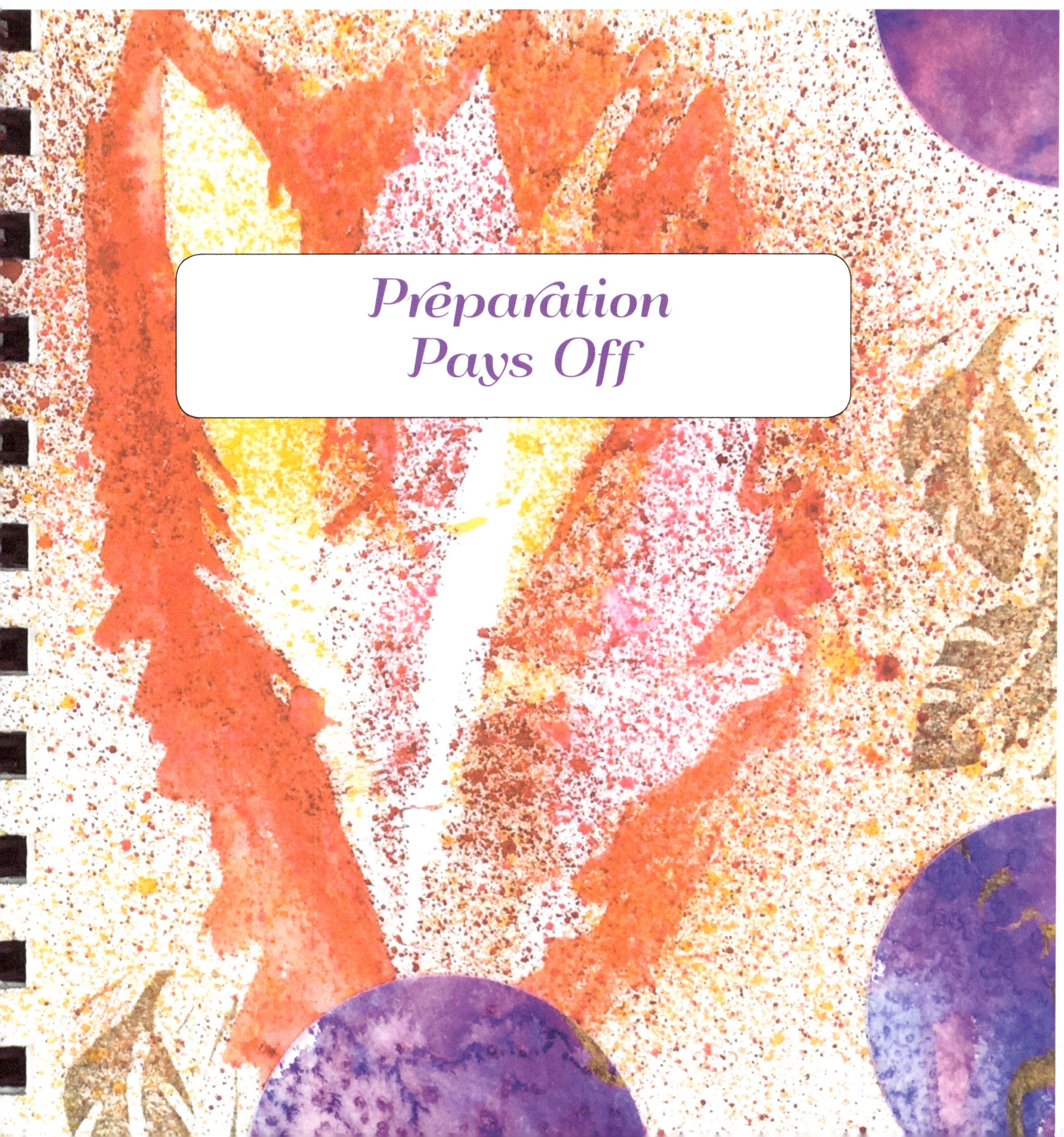
Preparation
Pays Off

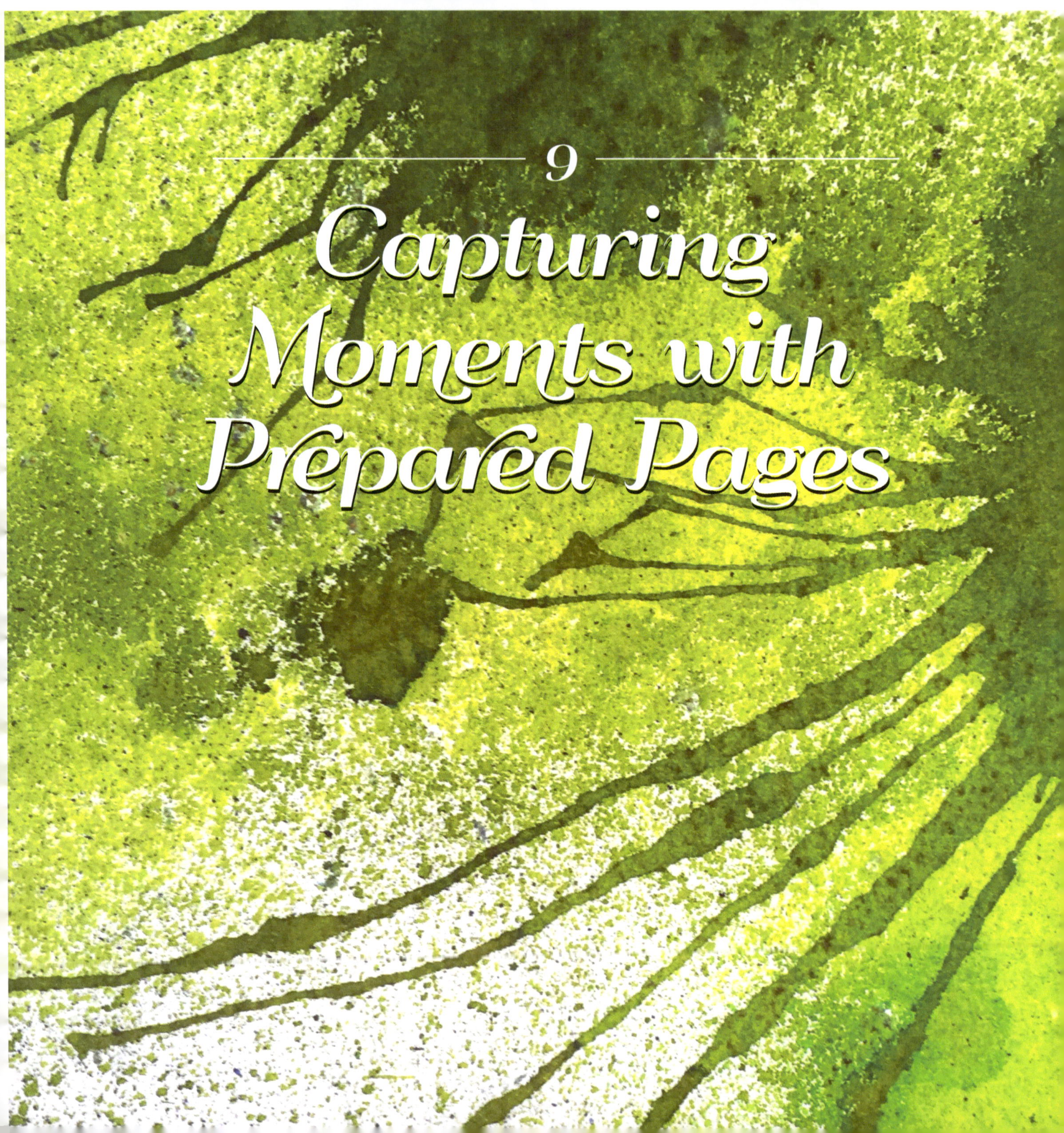
9
Capturing
Moments with
Prepared Pages

We spent the first eight chapters of this book setting ourselves up to find moments of joy and playing with a variety of techniques designed to get some life onto the blank pages in our art journals. Now what? Here is where the art journal practice gets interesting. With no rules to follow and encouragement to try the "what if" approach, it is time to consider what the stage is actually set for. What happens to make the art journal practice transform into joyful pages?

Materials

BASICS

- Art journal

FOCUS MATERIALS FOR THIS CHAPTER

- Comfy walking shoes
- Bag to carry your art journal and supplies
- Pens for writing (such as a Micron 005)
- Chalk set plus cotton rounds

"Your visions will become clear only when you can look into your own heart. Who looks outside, dreams; who looks inside, awakes."

C.G. Jung

My journals are used to capture moments. Sounds simple, and it is.

After pages are prepared, I will sometimes add a top layer of writing, taking a more traditional journal or diary approach. Or I might add a top layer of small illustrations to reflect some event in my life (usually a small interaction that I'd like to remember). I might glue down a business card or some odd piece of paper that has a tiny bit of meaning for that particular moment. Sometimes the prepared pages are satisfying just as they are and don't actually need anything else to give me pleasure. But since I like to use my journals to record my inner and outer experiences, I tend to use the pages as jumping-off points to play with ideas, thoughts and memories and to process work.

Sometimes I take my art journal (with the prepared pages) to meet up with a group of friends who also like journal work. We started by sitting around in a coffee shop but now meet in dive bars in Denver since there is always room for seven of us to sit at a table in the middle of the day. As we talk and laugh or sit quietly together, I capture moments and snippets of our conversations on the prepared pages. There is often something easy and interesting to sketch, or something silly to record. I love my dive bar art journal books as each page brings back a funny memory of my dive bar friends and our adventures.

Sometimes I need a jump-start on my journal page. My mind is blank, I have just a few minutes for something creative and I have a few art materials nearby calling my name.

Journal Prompt

With my journal open I'll start by sketching the glass of water on the table. While sketching, I am listening to the conversation and writing down phrases from the random, rambling conversations.

> *What do you see or hear right now that you can record in your journal?*

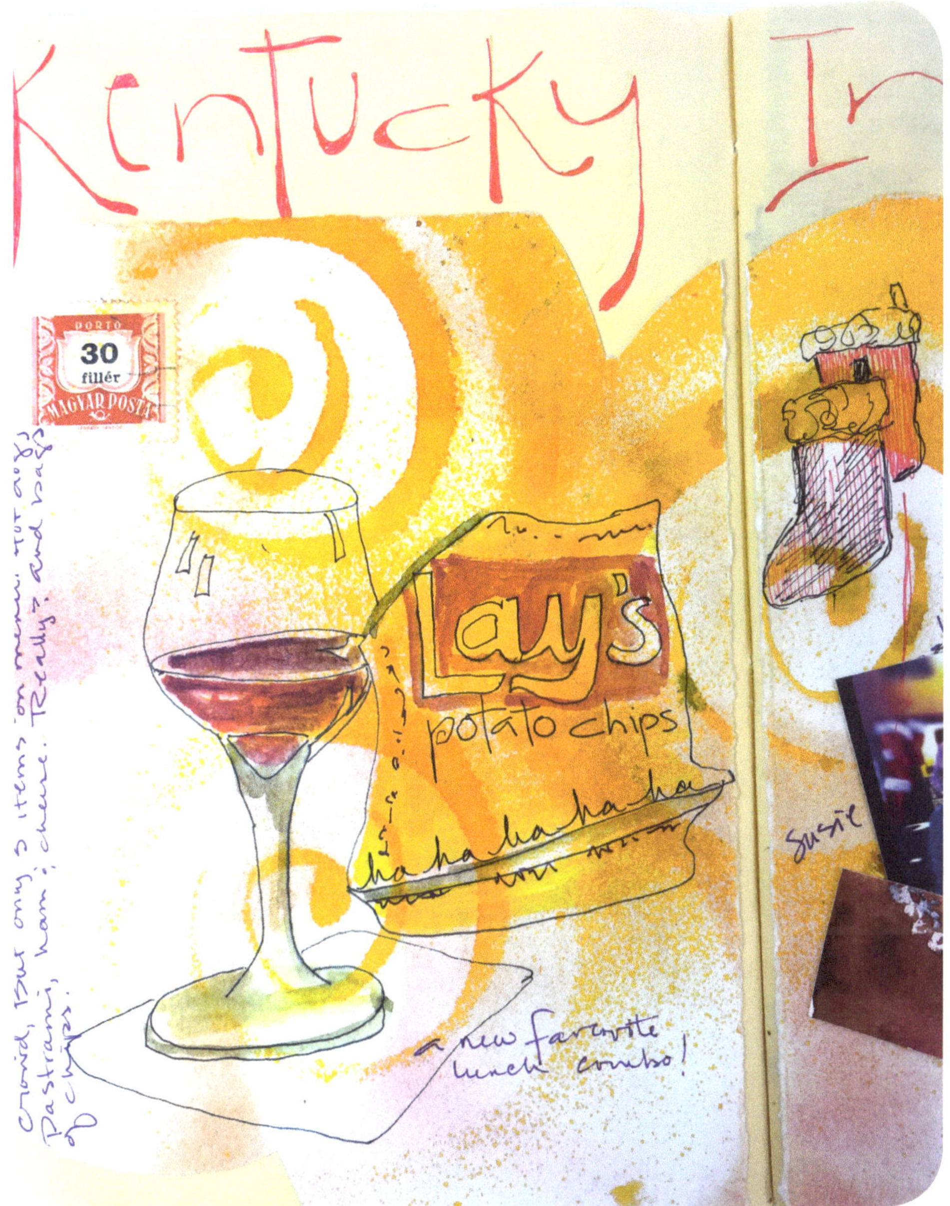

Pages prepared ahead of time with colorful ink sprays are the perfect backdrop for sketching when I'm out with my art journal group.

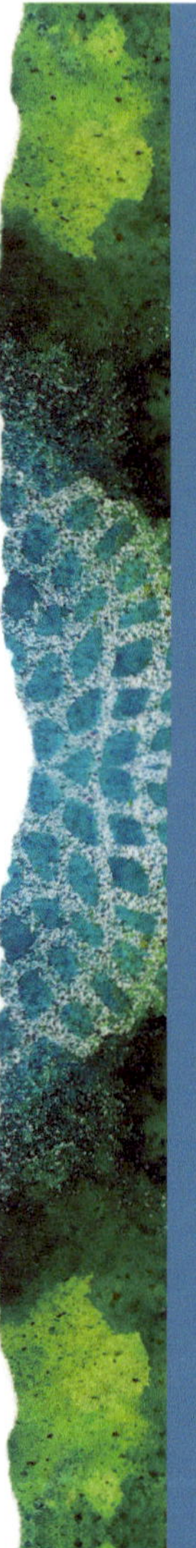

Six Go-To Journal Prompts

1. Series of Seven: What have I learned in the last seven days? What have I learned in the last seven weeks? What have I learned in the last seven months? (You can use any number; the point is to focus on what you have learned...)

2. What was the last thing I did that was the first time I ever did that?

3. Add a list. I keep a page in my art journal just for list topics. I have also shared the lists with my sister through texts, and have taken a screen shot then printed off the text my sister sends me with numerous, funny reasons for whatever we are talking about at the moment. I love attaching screen shots of texts to my journal pages.

4. Have you found a lovely leaf, interesting feather or a beautiful shell? Capture the moment by tracing around the object on top of an art journal page. I know, we think an alarm will go off if we trace, but why not? It can be really satisfying, and a dark black pen can give an interesting line on top of the ink blooms or the cray pas resist. You can fill in the traced shape with chalk (using the application method described in chapter 6) or watercolor. If you have traced something on top of the Dylusions spray inks, then a wet paintbrush will move the inks and make them look like watercolor compared to the spray pattern on the rest of the page.

5. Memory maps are another go-to favorite. I will often write all the places I had to get to earlier in the week, or during that day, and draw a rudimentary map using dotted lines and arrows to show the crazy movement paths I followed.

6. Try a calendar grid. If I find myself a bit lacking in the creative flow, I will set up a calendar of seven days or two weeks on a prepared page. Sometimes I use the chalk to define the days, scrubbing the chalk around small pieces of cut-up index cards. Then I'll go back and fill in the dates and the events. I find this very soothing and a quick way to find my way back to a creative zone.

I will open the art journal to a prepared page that seems to fit my mood and take a look at some of my favorite journal writing prompts to get me going.

I've included a few favorite prompts in this chapter. Some of these prompts are based on introspection; some are based on just remembering a crazy week. Some prompts spring from the funny conversations around me, some come from inner dialogues.

In the Wild

Some of my best art journal flow experiences are when I take my journal for a date. I grab comfy shoes and put my book in a bag with a few pens and my debit card. Off I go to a place I will feel comfortable sitting quietly alone for a while (park bench, coffee shop, bookstore, museum). It may take a few minutes to adjust to being in public with my colorful pages wide open, but I can pretty quickly put on the cloak of invisibility and sink my focus onto a page. Sketching or writing, it does not matter. I am basically just trying to keep the pages alive with some thoughts, some energy. Talk about time standing still: I now know to set my phone alarm as an hour can fly by in just a few minutes. Here is where concentration meets skill. I can write on top of prepared pages, or sketch on prepared pages, or start a brand new

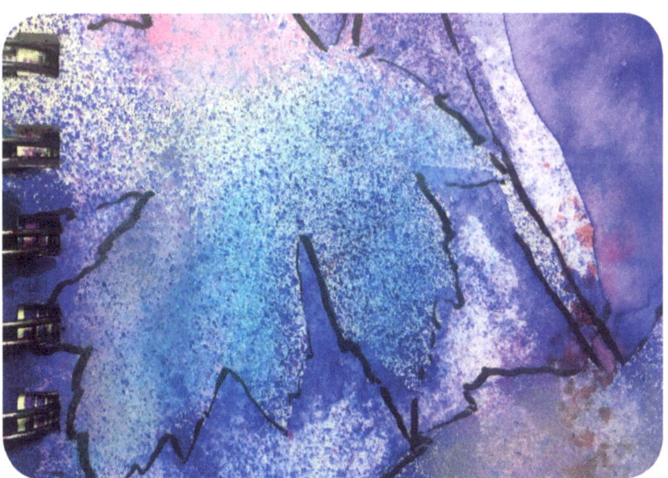

Try tracing a leaf, shell or other item your find onto a prepared page with a black pen.

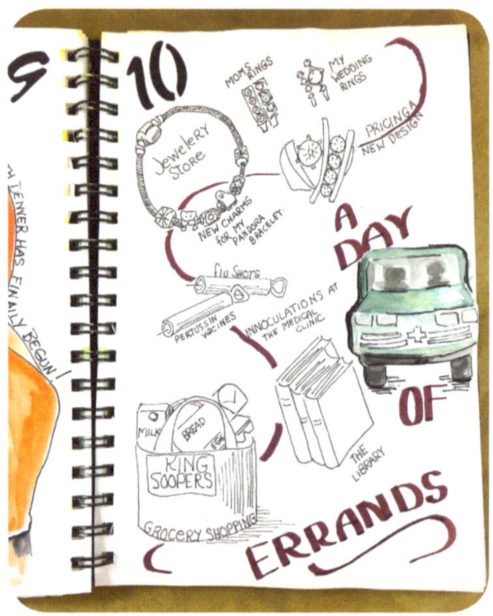
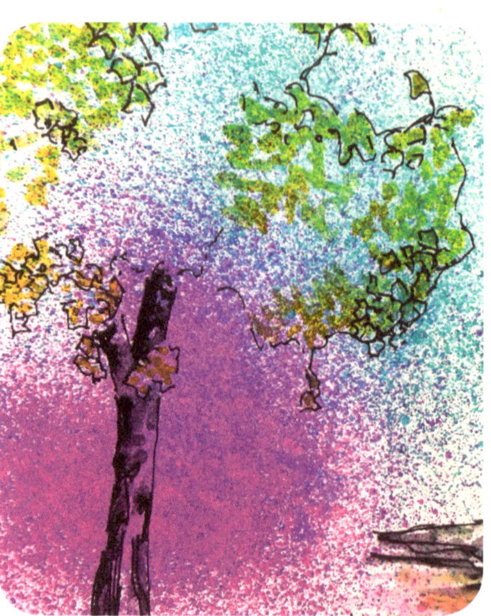

When she couldn't think of what to write, Joyce Breheny journaled about her day in a mix of words and sketches.

A spray of ink becomes a vibrant tree with the addition of a pen sketch.

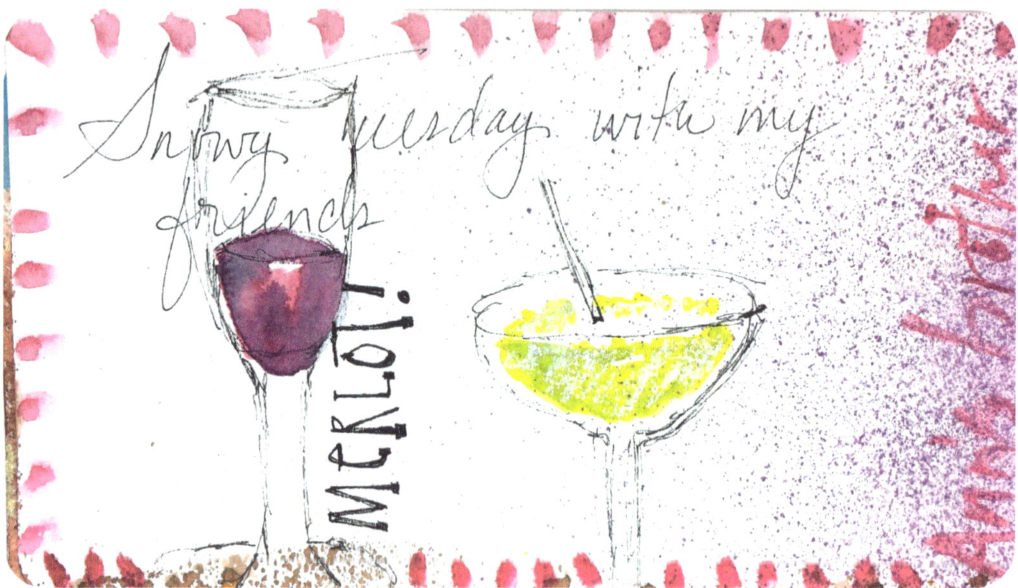

Capturing small moments, simple joys or things to be thankful for is a great way to fill your art journal.

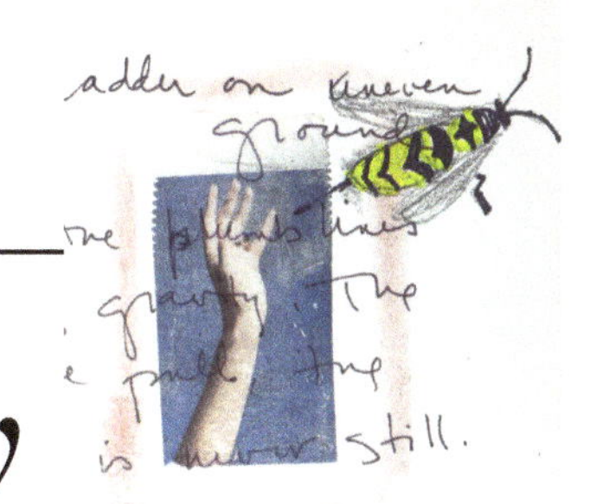

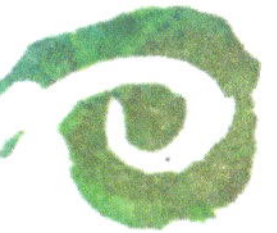

Buzz Worthy

A few years ago I had a friend tell me about being stung by a swarm of wasps while she was doing yard work near an outdoor shed. I was so upset by her description that I dreamt of wasps that night. The very next day, no kidding, I put on a garden glove and was instantly stung right on the palm of my hand by a wasp that had been hiding in the dark glove. This was crazy! After the pain and shock subsided, I looked up images of wasps and spent the rest of the summer working with sketches and collages of these annoying creatures.

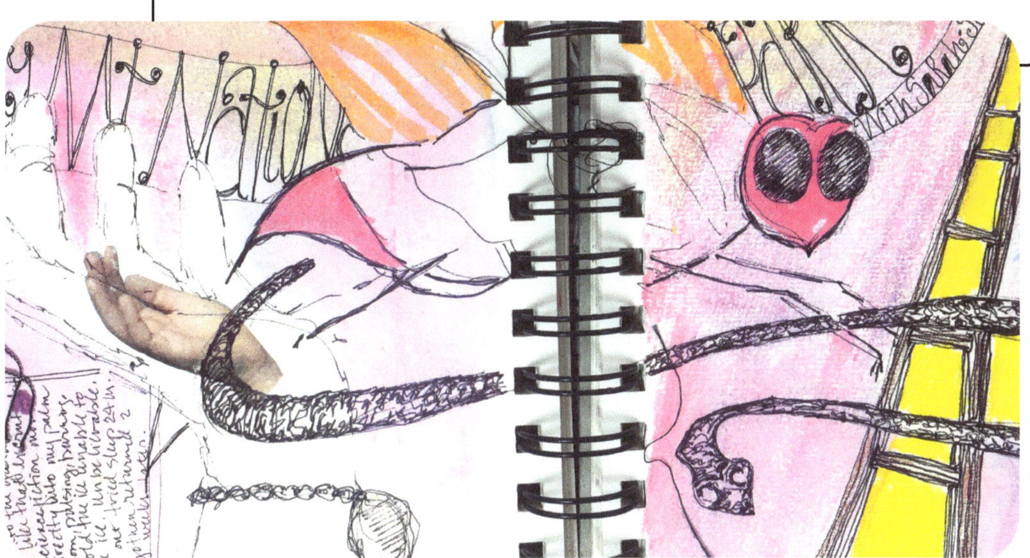

A real-life event, a dream or a new discovery can all lead to interesting art journal entries.

page with something glued down. It is joyful
and cathartic and calming and energizing. It is
art journaling in the zone.

Bringing a small journal and just a pen
or two on a hike is another soul-balm. I am
fortunate to live in a beautiful part of the
planet with access to grand vistas. I can find
a comfy rock, breathe deep and pull out my
journal. I will work on pages that might have
been prepared many days earlier and just try
to record the moment using words or a quick
sketch. When I look back in the journal long
after the hike I am often brought back to the
peaceful place and the joy-filled pages.

The most important message of this whole
book? Get some love on your pages. Breathe
life into your book. Let yourself play with
delightful art materials and explore them in
new ways with no limitations.

That creative zone is just next to your comfort zone, and those little zones of delight are
embedded within; I welcome you to step out
a bit and find your flow. It is worth the trip!

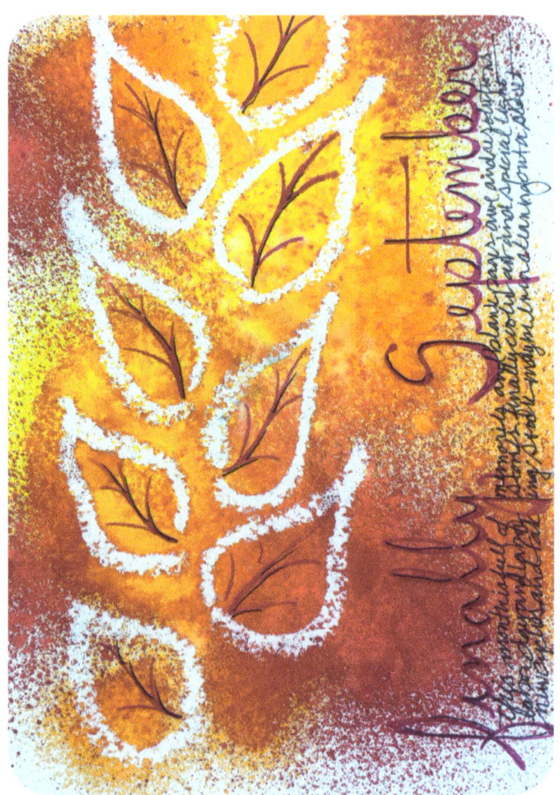

*What will the colors and marks in your art journal suggest
to you?*

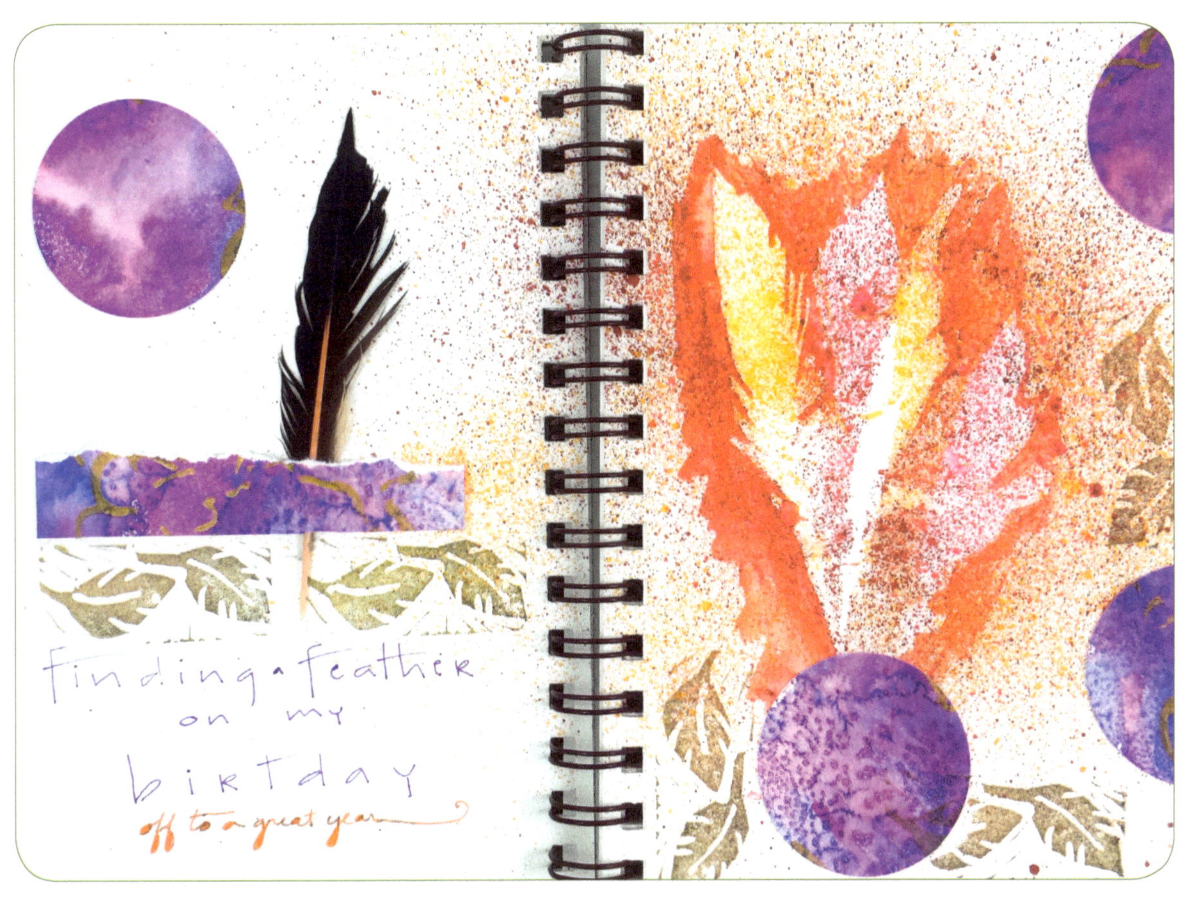

"*Vulnerability is the birthplace of innovation, creativity and change.*"
Brené Brown

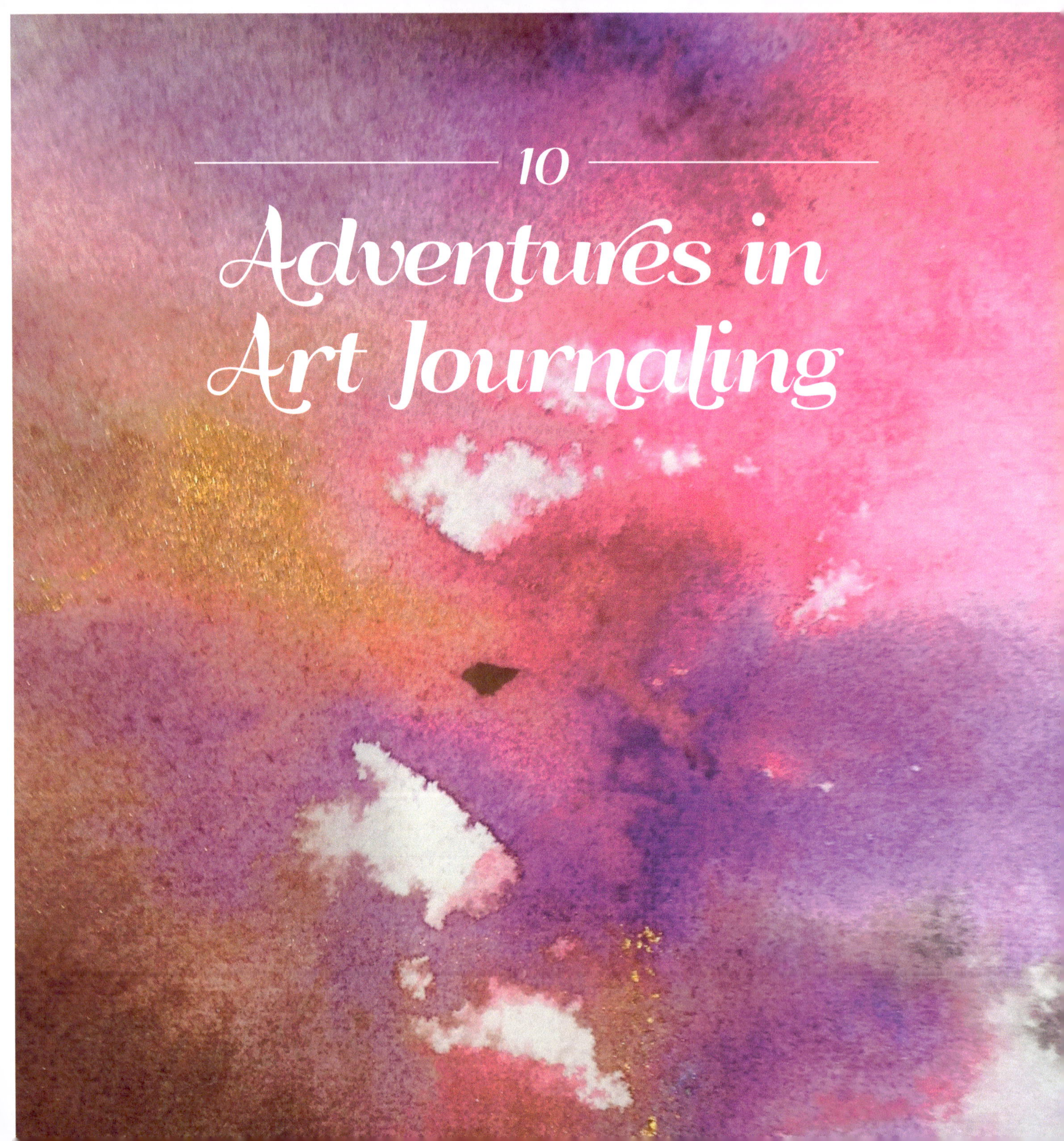

10
Adventures in
Art Journaling

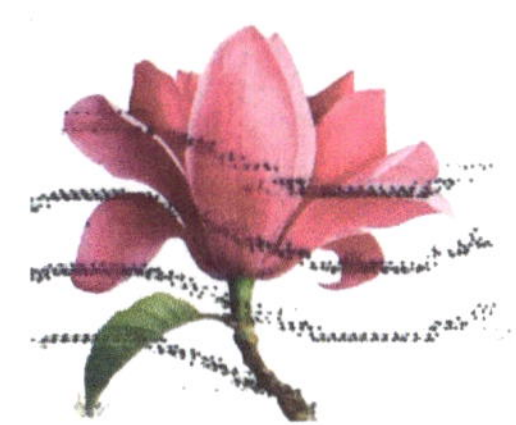

Over

time, my art journal takes on a life of its own. As I turn the pages over and over, and fill pages over the course of a few months, I can sense a theme emerge and I look for meaning. This is a vague concept; I know it when I feel it. The theme might be a phrase, a word or an overall concept. Sometimes I don't sense a theme until I am almost finished with the journal after having built layers and textures on various pages. Sometimes the theme starts to emerge when I am about half way through the book, and then it is interesting to see if the remaining pages somehow fit.

When I am close to finishing the art journal, I like to excavate or review the pages to look for the theme if one has not already presented itself. To excavate my book, I turn the pages slowly and look for a juicy phrase, or a word that keeps cropping up or just grabs my attention. Excavating the journal is the slow and intentional look at each page that allows me to see the journal as a

Materials

BASICS
- **Your art journal**
- **Supplies used in previous chapters**
- **White gesso (optional)**

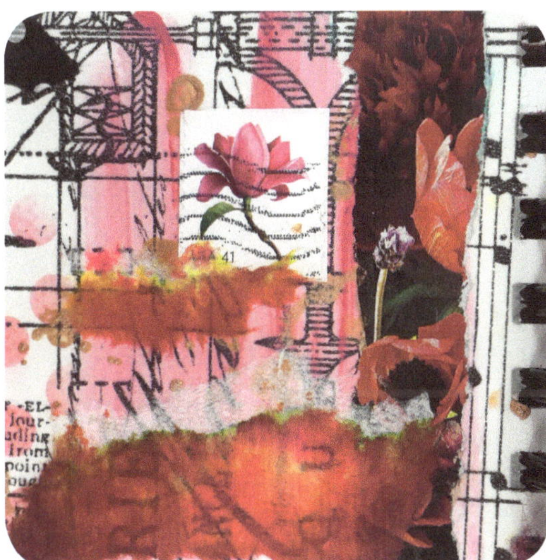

This detail from a collage by Debra Gust shows multiple layers; rubber stamp, ink, paper towels, postage stamp and a bit of decorative paper.

total package, a series of moments making a whole. Sometimes the excavation does not end in a single word or phrase, but gets me thinking about the months it has taken to fill the pages. Where have I been? What has occupied my head and heart? What moments stand out? What moments were little gems along my path? It is from this review process that I will determine what to name this art journal.

The easiest way to add a title (plus the dates) to your art journal is to embellish a large shipping tag (or similar shape) and hang it from the coil spine. You can also create your own tag by cutting a rectangle shape out of your mixed media practice paper (decorated or plain). Then punch a hole in the narrow end and add a ribbon or string. By now, you are familiar with a variety of techniques that could work to embellish the tag:

- Spray it with India ink using a commercial stencil
- Spray it with Dylusions ink (using a commercial stencil or found-object mask)
- Use the Tombow Dual Brush pen for hand lettering
- Use the Pigma Brush pen for hand lettering
- Use rubber stamps to create a border around the lettering
- Use the rubber stamp inkpad, rubbed around the edges of the tag, to make the edges darker
- Use the chalk pastels (applied with cotton squares) to add color to the tag

Finishing touch: I have completed a zillion art journal books over the course of the 20 years I have been creating joyful pages. They present a challenge to store. Adding a tag to the spine helps me to line them up by date. I also love how the line of tags looks on my studio shelves.

Why stop at just adding tags? Uh-oh, here is a Pandora's box worth opening. After hanging the title tag, go ahead and add all kinds of lovely

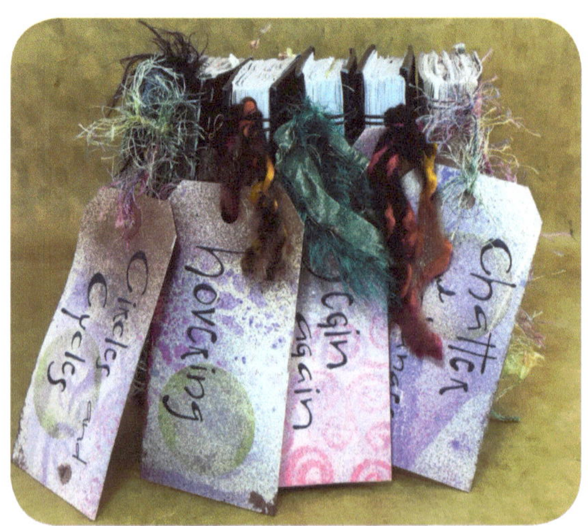

White tags colored with sprayed inks, stencils and chalks can be labeled to help identify your finished art journals.

Step by Step by Step

While I was working on a journal a few years ago I also started training to walk a half marathon as a way to celebrate a (big) birthday. Many of my pages reflected all the unexpected adventures I had while training for the long 13.1 miles of the race. I walked and mused about this particular art journal every day. One day on a training walk, I felt my ankle turn and I realized the book should be titled "Uneven Ground" which had metaphoric meaning as well as a direct reference to the many miles on varied surfaces I had covered.

And speaking of long journeys, I can't tell you how often I am asked, "How long does it take to fill your art journal?" No kidding; I have actually kept track; it is most often a nine-month process, and I am not making that up!

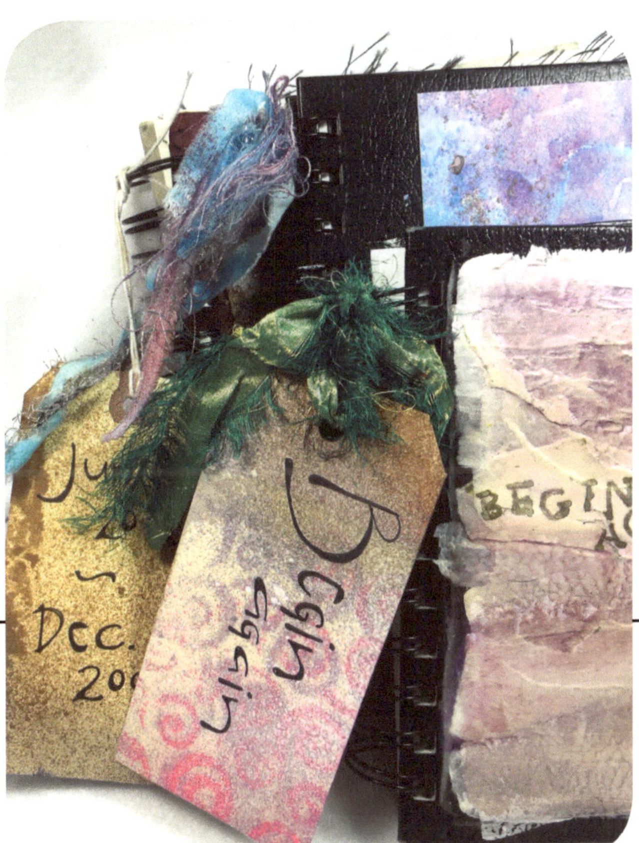

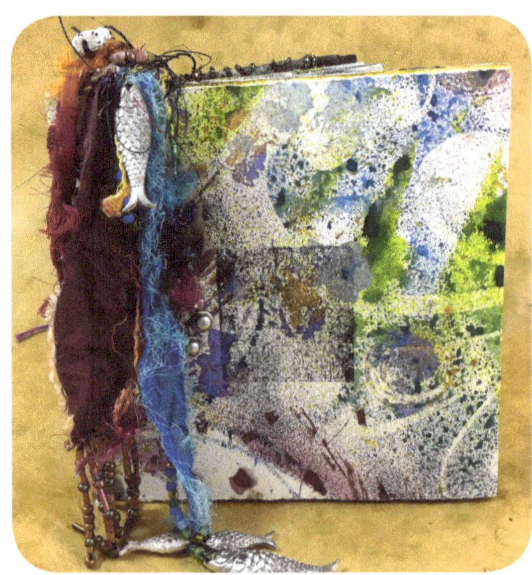

Diana Roth made a book cover out of a practice page sprayed with inks, then added a fabulous spine of sari silk and charms.

Finished pages are a delight to see and touch. Ann Williams attached a shimmery flower-shaped disc to a page filled with layers.

beads and charms—anything that gives you pleasure. I have used decorative wires, ribbons, embroidery floss, kitchen string—anything to get the beads and gewgaws hung.

Mixing your media on the spine is so wonderful; your hands will twitch when you see the dangly, crazy things and you will barely be able to leave your art journal alone on the shelf for long.

Now that you are well on your way to filling your pages with joy and you have experienced the amazingly powerful creative zone or flow that you can enter by spraying, spritzing, dripping, rubbing and generally playing with a pile of delightful art materials, you are ready to think about making this activity a real practice.

Joyful Pages in Real Life

To make any new habit into a practice takes time and repetition. There will be challenges to your time and your enthusiasm for sure. But there are a few tricks I have found to be helpful:

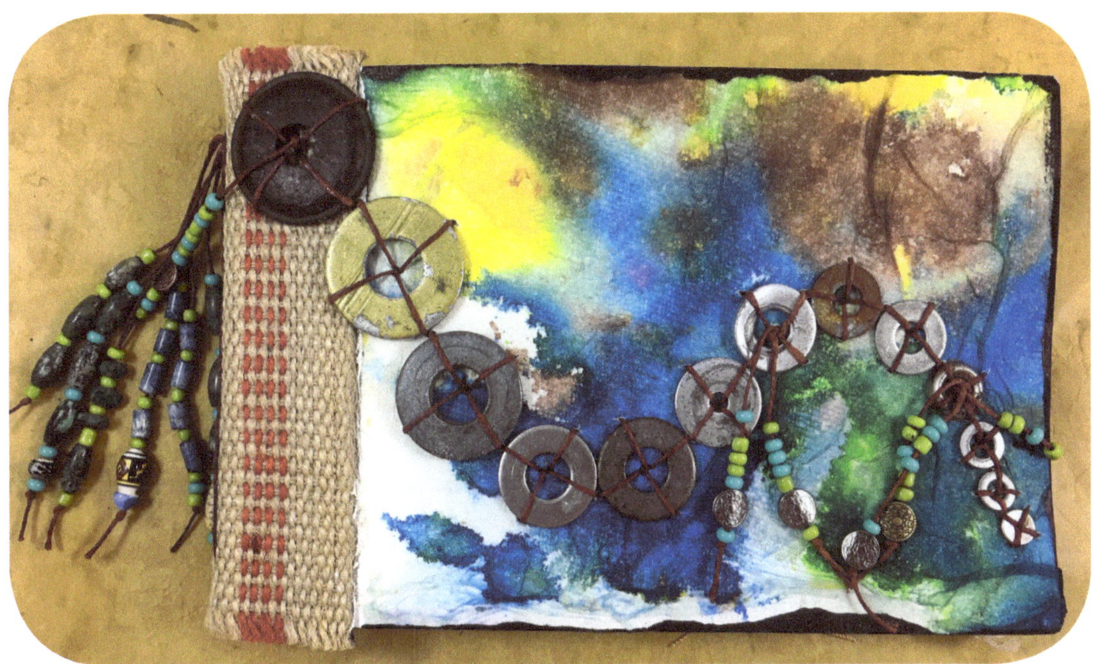

Jennifer Evans glued an ink-stained paper towel to the cover of a journal, then added other found objects.

1. Find a child, spouse or friends who might be willing to explore their own creative zone alongside you. Working in art journals together is a marvelous way to share sacred space; a quiet zone but also a zone full of laughter and playfulness. Create an art journal group with regular meetings. I think a group offers the strongest motivation.

2. Consider taking an art journal workshop or attending an art journal retreat. You will meet other folks who are dedicated to their creative zone efforts and learn new techniques. As an art journal instructor, I can say that some of the most delightful hours have been spent with playful students willing to embark on this adventure together. I have learned from them in each class. I have also seen a number of wonderful art journal groups form as a result of the connections students have made in the class. Some of these groups are still meeting after a decade.

3. Open your calendar and make some art journal dates with yourself. Seriously. Put it in writing that you are going to spend one hour a month (hopefully more) doing something you love. Then stick to it. Either pull out all of your materials or take your journal to a coffee shop, on a hike or other spot with a nice bench.

4. If you have a busy, crazy carpool schedule then keep a little bag in your minivan with

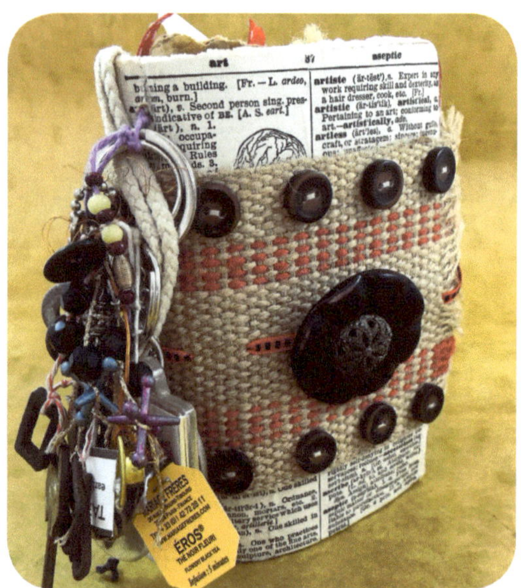

Jennifer Evans created a journal, wrapped the book in a dictionary page then a piece of burlap (with buttons sewn on), then went crazy with attaching found objects to the spine.

some basic supplies. It never hurts to get to your destination a bit early so you can work on a journal page from the driver's seat. This is where prepared pages are great; you can do those at home, and then add text when you are out and about.

5. Finally, start where you are. Journal about your crazy-busy schedule or a time of transition. Don't wait for stars to align; instead, I hope that you will see the benefit of letting go and facing the WPA (white page anxiety) with courage, joy and an adventurous attitude.

I do believe that getting into our creative zone is rejuvenating and calming. It has to have positive health effects. I know for sure that flow can be joyous and delightful, and stepping away from our daily grind can give us perspective and clarity. Cultivating curiosity is synonymous with taking an adventurous approach; focusing on the value of the process over a perfect product makes room for joyful pages.

I encourage you to watch the ink bloom and the sprays mingle with that sense of delight in the moment. You are invited to give yourself permission to leave any expectations of perfection at the door and enter your creative zone with me.

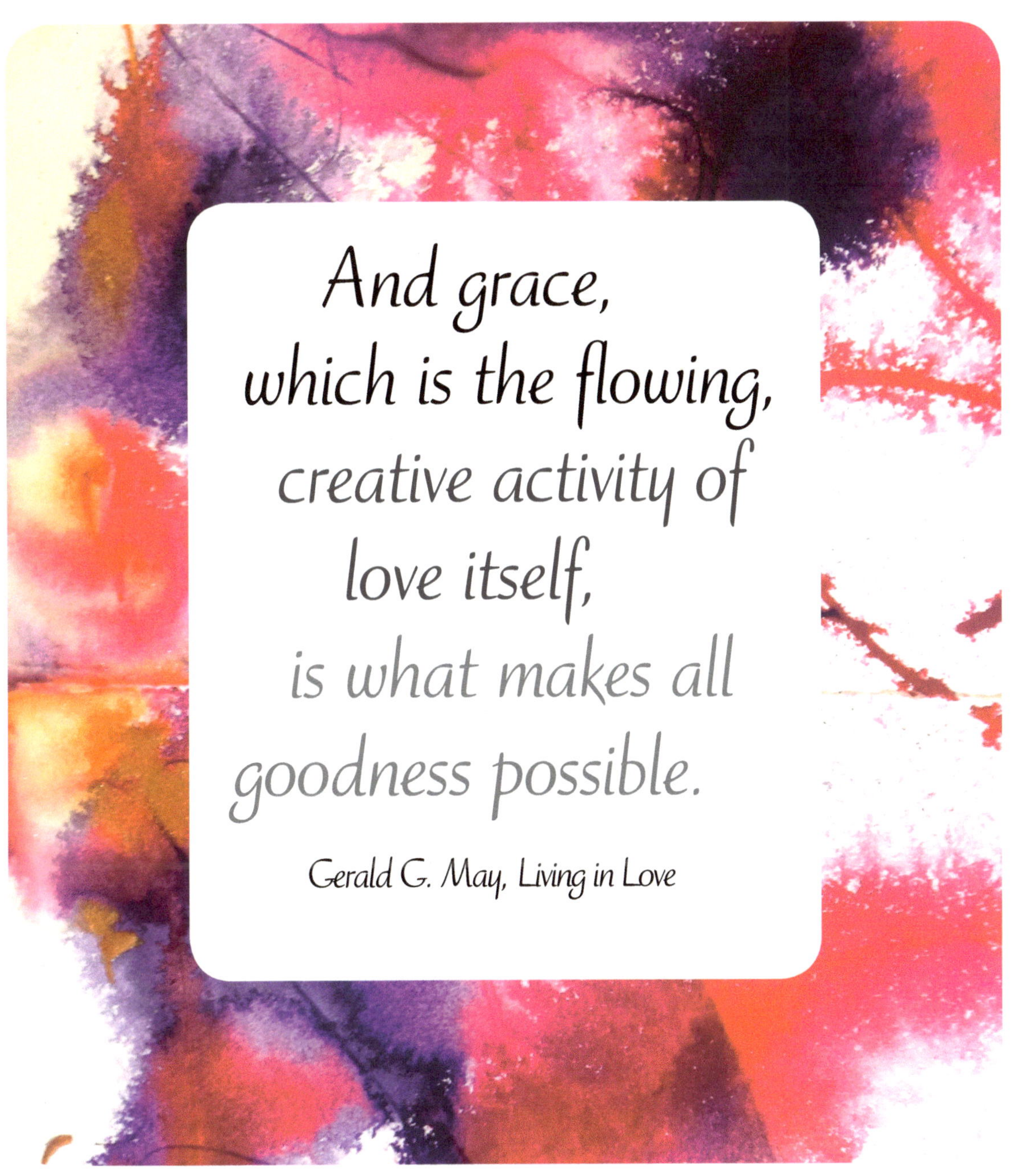

And grace,
which is the flowing,
creative activity of
love itself,
is what makes all
goodness possible.

Gerald G. May, Living in Love

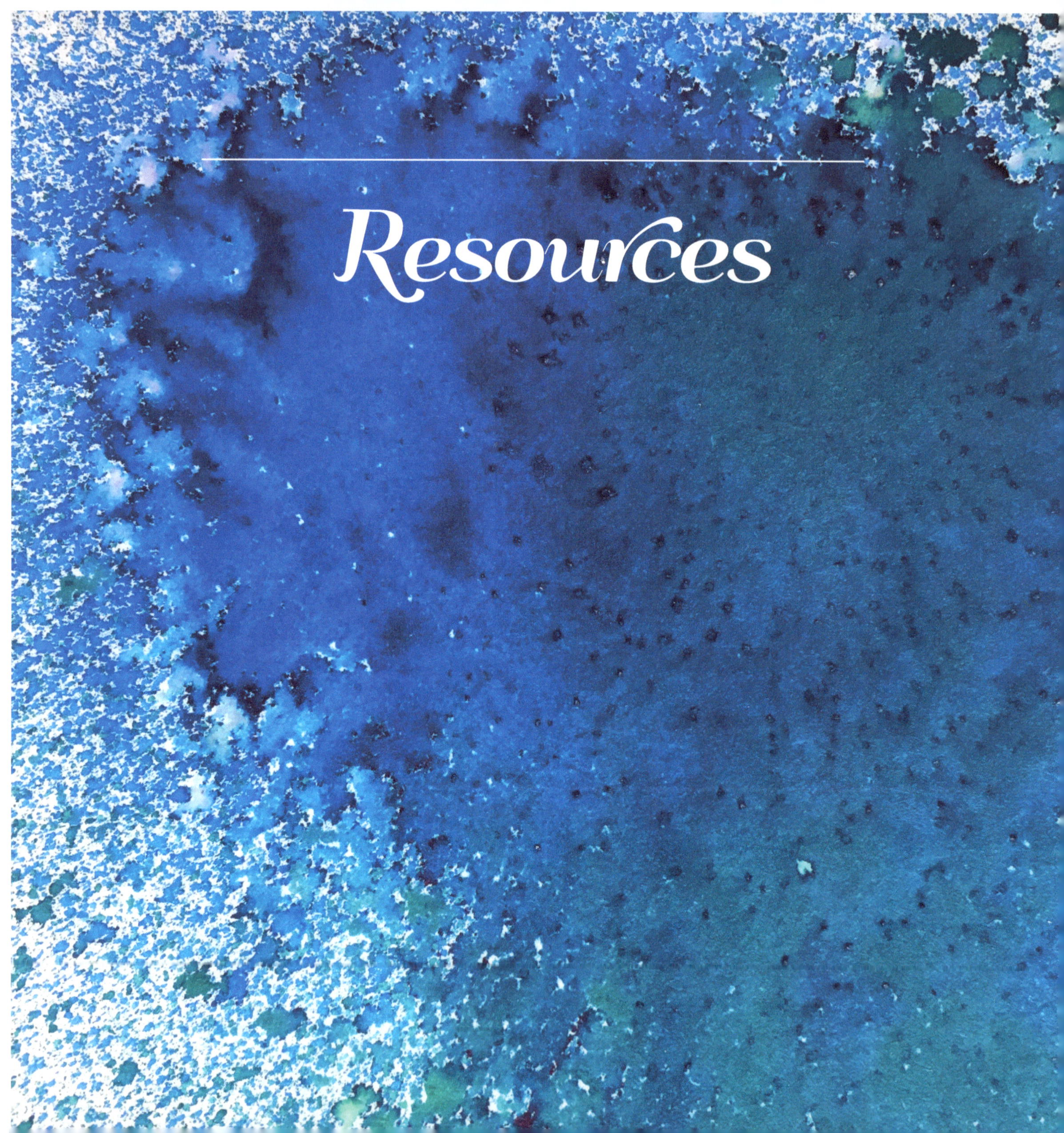

Resources

Supplies

SKETCH BOOKS AND PAPER PADS:

Aquabee
www.beepaper.com

Canson
en.canson.com

Strathmore
www.strathmoreartist.com

INKS:

Dr. Ph. Martin's Bombay India ink
www.docmartins.com; 800-843-8293

Dylusions
www.rangerink.com; 732-389-3535

PENS:

Pigma Micron pens
www.sakuraofamerica.com

Tombow Dual Brush
www.tombowusa.com; 800-835-3232

CHALK PASTELS:

Faber-Castell
www.fabercastell.com; 800-311-8684

STENCILS:

The Crafters Workshop
www.thecraftersworkshop.com

StencilGirl Products
www.stencilgirlproducts.com

INKPADS:

Distress
www.rangerink.com; 732-389-3535

Memento and Versamark
www.tsukineko.co.jp/english/

Color Box
www.clearsnap.com; 800-448-4862

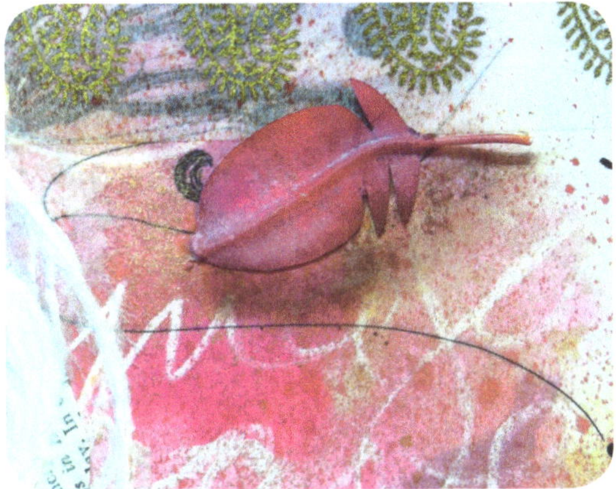

I attached a feather coated with ink to this journal page, which features stamps, spray and resist techniques.

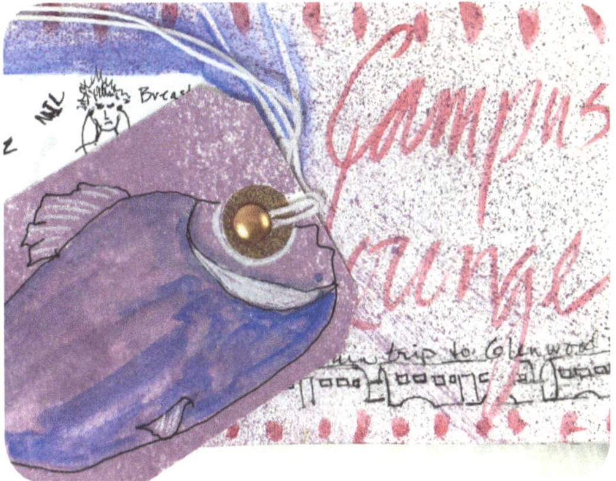

A shipping tag, attached with a fastener, is an interactive element on this page in one of my dive-bar journals.

One of the most efficient ways to share information with my students about the supplies I use during an art journal workshop is to direct them to my Pinterest page. I invite you to visit www.pinterest.com/jcmamet.

On this page, you will see a "Materials and Tools I Love" board. After you click this board, you will see small images of all the supplies mentioned in this book plus many more. If you are interested in details (price, online sources, etc.) just click the image twice and you will be directed to a retail site. Please note, I am not endorsing any particular online site, just offering this method as a convenient way to find the products.

Denver is fortunate to have two independent art stores. Guiry's Color Source (www.guirys.com) carries all of the Dylusions sprays mentioned in this book as well as all of the other materials. Meininger has a full range of art supplies (www.meininger.com).

If I am shopping online I usually compare the prices for art materials between the following sites:

• Dick Blick (www.dickblick.com)
• Jerry's Artarama (www.jerrysartarama.com)
• Amazon (www.amazon.com)

Additionally, I publish a monthly e-newsletter with tips and tricks for art journaling, travel journaling and sketching. I often review products, books and websites. You can sign up for the monthly newsletter on my website contact page: www.jcmamet.net/contact. You can view archived newsletters at www.jcmamet.net/newsletters.

Helpful Tutorials

Over the past few years I have posted a number of video tutorials on YouTube. It is easy to find each of the titles listed below by entering Judith Cassel-Mamet in the search area of the YouTube home page (www.youtube.com).

• How to Begin a Mixed Media Journal
• How to Personalize Your Journal Cover
• Altered Photos for Adventure Journals
• Image Transfer Process Using Tape
• How to Use Dustless Blending Chalk in Mixed Media Journals
• Visual Journals: Shaped Pages
• Crested Butte Simple Sketch Postcard (and Demo)

Further Reading

Some of my favorite books are listed here. I have divided them into books that address creativity and flow, books that I like from the world of art journaling, two that highlight specific techniques, and one book that started me on the path to writing *Joyful Pages*.

Creativity and Flow

Art and Fear, David Bayles and Ted Orland (1993, Image Continuum Press)

This was required reading for all of the University of Denver classes I taught. It is one of my all-time favorites because the authors ask key questions about the motivation to create, the issues that accompany the act of creating and the ways we sabotage our creative process. It is a timeless, simple book that appeals to both my heart and head.

Creativity: Flow and the Psychology of Discovery and Invention, Mihaly Csikszentmihalyi (1996, HarperCollins Publishers)

Csikszentmihalyi opened the academic world to the study of creativity as a unique and valuable field. While the research is over 20 years old, the impact of his work is still applicable to anyone interested in a broad view of creative expression.

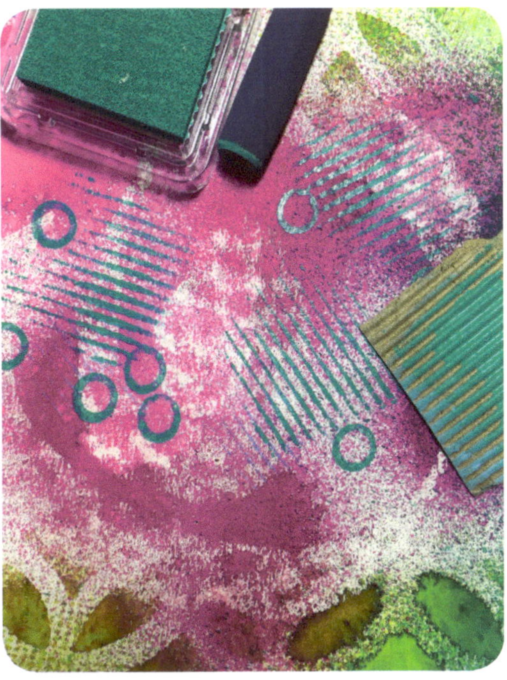

Raid your junk drawer or recycling bin for "found" stamps like pencil grips or pieces of corrugated cardboard.

Your Creative Brain, Shelley Carson, PhD (2010, Harvard University Press)

Dr. Carson's research on how our brains respond to creativity will rock your world! She moved the concept of the split-brain theory (right versus left brain) into the 21st century. This sounds like a thick technical tome but it is readable and geared to the non-medical, curious reader.

Creative is a Verb, Patti Digh (2011, Morris Book Publishing Company)

"If you're alive you're creative" is Digh's mantra. She has created a wonderful book, jam-packed with prompts, encouragement and purely fun exercises.

Art Journaling

The Decorated Page, Gwen Diehn (2002, Lark Books)

This is one of the first books that addressed the art journaling approach that I found myself embracing. I used this as a required reading for my university classes, loving Diehn's gentle guidance and clear directions.

Inner Hero, Creative Art Journal, Quinn McDonald (2013, North Light Books)

The author offers some great prompts for art journalers who need to silence their inner critic.

Recommended References for Joyful Journaling

The Art of Whimsical Lettering, Joanne Sharpe (2014, Interweave)

Sharpe shows us how to use our own handwriting in a joyful manner and gives great examples for using text as a graphic, decorative element.

Making an Impression, Geninne D. Zlatkis (2012, Lark Books)

A beautiful book about carving your own stamps.

My Greatest Inspiration

Stupendous Stitching, Carol Ann Waugh (2012, Xcellent Press)

If you are exploring mixed media, and loving the mountain of materials that are possible to use in an art journal, then you will love this book. Stitching creates fabulous texture and Carol Waugh is a master of "Stupendous Stitching." She is also one of the most generous artists I know and has shared her publication efforts with many of her devoted followers.

Additional Inspiration

It would be possible to spend so much time looking at creative websites, Pinterest pages and Etsy sites that there would not be time to open a journal and actually do something. If I could only have one online site to visit for inspiration in the creative process it would be Nicholas Wilton's website and blog at www.nicholaswilton.com. He is a painter, thinker and one of the most generous online presences I have found.

Acknowledgments

My husband, Sam, is the glue behind the scenes. He has accommodated my workshop schedule and helped me carry 9 million tons of art materials, all with love and good humor. Elliot and Abe (my sons) offered unwavering support and creative insights. Thanks to these three for never seeming to mind when we could not open the washing machine because my art supplies needed another surface and I spilled out of my studio.

Thank you to my mentor, Carol Ann Waugh, who challenged, encouraged and shared lots of red wine along the way.

My sister Robin has held me steady and kept my vision alive. She is the most creative person I know.

My Dive Bar Journal group has been the core of my creative community; oh man, do we laugh.

And to all of my students in Denver, Taos, Paonia, Crested Butte and on both coasts: Wow! You inspire me. I am connected to all of my teachers, and my students, in gratitude. Sharing the creative zone weaves our lives together. I send love and appreciation to all of you who show up, show courage and show your playful spirit.

Thank you to the artists who contributed their work to this book: Joyce Breheny, Susan Coombe, Jennifer Evans (Jennifer@tankersly.com), Debra Gust (debragust@gmail.com), Diana Roth (Diana.pinondesign@comcast.net) and Ann Williams.

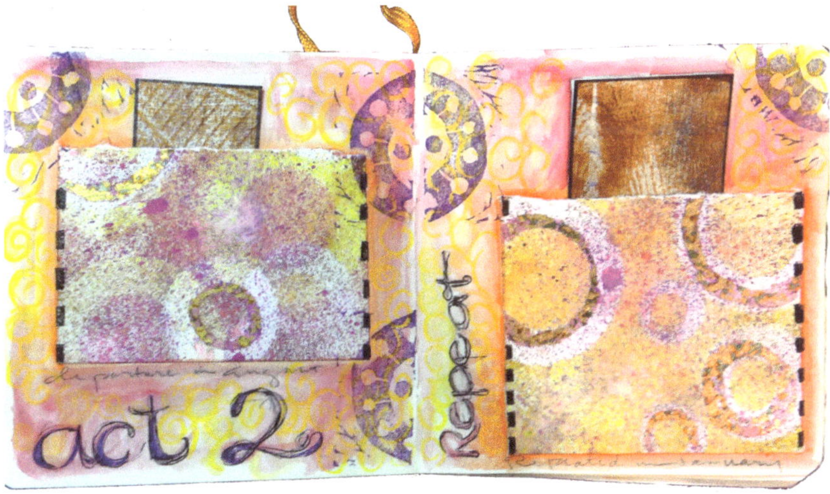

Pockets made of paper rectangles hold treasures inside this journal spread.

About the Author

Judith Cassel-Mamet has always been inspired by a well-told story, wild clouds, aspen forests and wide-open vistas. She began her art education career at Englewood High School (outside of Denver, Colorado). She went on to teach creative expression at the University of Denver for 10 years while she developed a passion for mixed media painting and art journaling. Judith currently teaches at the Art Student League of Denver and independently. She offers workshops and art retreats for art journaling and mixed media work in a variety of fantastic spots, including Taos, New Mexico, New York City, Crested Butte and Paonia, Colorado, and Barcelona, Spain. Judith has shown her mixed media work in various galleries in Denver and Crested Butte.

Judith offers a monthly "Adventure Journal Newsletter" with free tips and tricks for journaling and sketching. Visit her website to sign up for the newsletter, view a gallery of her work and to find information about upcoming classes.

www.jcmamet.net

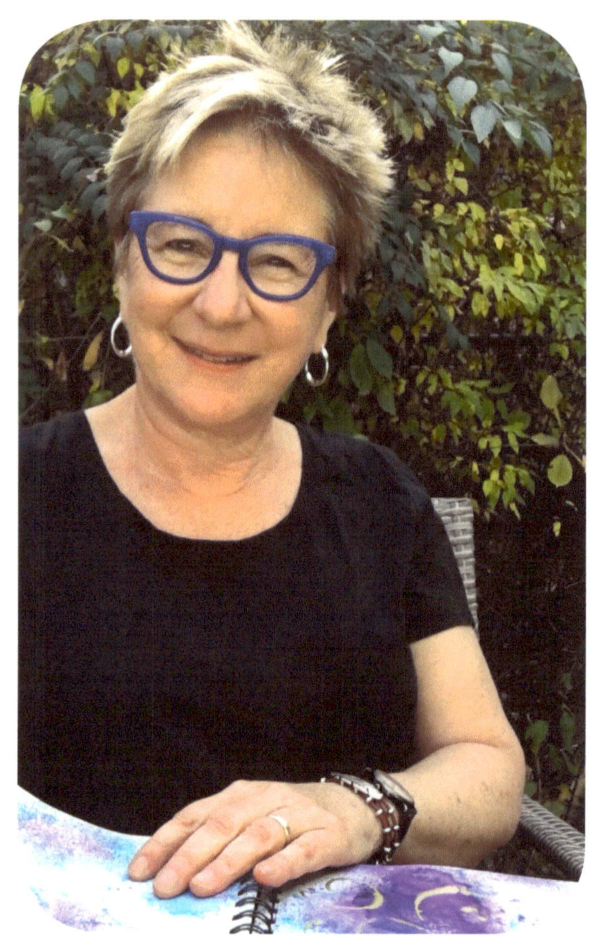

www.ingramcontent.com/pod-product-compliance
Lightning Source LLC
Chambersburg PA
CBHW042148030726

47599CB00004B/655